HOW GREEN WAS OUR WAVE

THE DAWN OF SURFING IN IRELAND

Kevin Cavey

 www.trafford.com

North America & international
toll-free: 844-688-6899 (USA & Canada)
fax: 812 355 4082

ACKNOWLEDGEMENTS

I would like to thank the families and friends of those great people who have surfed and loved, and gallantly passed into the hands of God. But also, to encourage those remaining who still foster the spirit of adventure that prevailed in the golden years to continue in that pursuit, and share with others as they do so!

Also, to thank the following for their advice, support, photographs and comical recollections:

Articles and comments: Roci Allan, Brian and Barry Britton, Ger Byrne, Ioni Byrne, Colm Cavey, Gerry Collins, Jurek Delimata, Henrietta Glendon, John Guinan, Maureen Gleeson, Patrick Kinsella, Zoe Lally, Martin Lloyd, Eamon Matthews, Mike Murphy, Joe Mc Govern, Sam McCrum, John McCarthy, Kevin Naughton, Antoin O'Looney, Hugh O'Brien-Moran, Alan Rich, Roger Steadman, Rodney Sumpter, Eddie Stewart, Bo Vance,

Readers: Conor Burns, Ann Cavey, Georgina Cavey, Tim Ferguson.

Editing: Alex and Jurek Delimata, Simon Coury.

Historical information: Brian Britton, Colm Cavey, Dave Kenny, Carmel Evans, Hugh O'Brien-Moran, Eric Randal, Joe Roddy.

Photographs: Archives of the Irish Surfing Association, Easkey Britton, Naomi Britton, Gerard Byrne, Alan Duke, Davy Govan, Mike Heary, Ian Hill, Tony Lynch, Eamon Matthews, John McCarthy, Nobby Redman, Hugh O'Brien-Moran, Tom O'Brien, Alan Rich, Bo Vance.

Moral Support: Ann, Paul and Georgina Cavey and Carolyn Thornton.

In appreciation: Gerry Collins, Derek Moody and Ken Costigan of the Great Outdoors, Chatham Street and Clarendon Street, Dublin 2, who are the sponsors of this book.

Kevin Cavey

kevin.cavey@gmail.com

To my wife Ann whose beauty, I endlessly
perceive in the heaving ocean.

SPONSORS

Sean Duggan, Sweet Fancy Productions, Brooklyn, NY 11215. seanduggan01@gmail.com

The Irish Surfing Association, Easkey, Co Sligo. Tel 096-49429. www.isasurf.ie

The Great Outdoors, Chatham St, Dublin 2. Tel 01-6794293. www.greatoutdoors.ie

Lahinch Surf Shop, Lahinch, Co Clare. Tel 065 – 7081543. www. lahinchsurfshop.com

T Bay Surf Club. Tramore, Co. Waterford. info@tbaysurfclub.ie

T Bay Surf and Eco Centre, Tramore, Co Waterford. Tel 051 -391297 www.tbaysurf.com

Finn Mc Cools Surf School, Rossnowlagh, Co Donegal. 071 9859020. finmccools@gmail.com

Fin Mc Cools Surf Co. Green St, Dingle, Co Kerry. Tel 066 – 9150833. www.finmccools.ie

Bundoran Surf Co. Main St, Bundoran, Co Donegal. Tel 071 – 9841968. www.bundoransurfco.comhop.co.uk

Troggs Surf Shop, Main St, Portrush, Co Antrim. Tel +44 (0) 2870825476 www.troggssurfs

Incide Surf Shop, Bridge St, Cork City. Tel. 021 – 4505077. www. facebook.com/incide

River Deep Mountain High, The Corn Store, Middle St, Galway City. Tel 091 – 563938 www.rdmh.ie

Surf Mountain, Lisburn Co Antrim and Bangor Co Down, Tel+44 (0) – 28914588 www.surfmountain.

CONTENTS

INTRODUCTION

Ireland of the 1950s seemed to be a mixture of Georgian architecture, green buses, windy weather, turf smoke, sunshine and good-humoured people. Across the landscape were twisted roads, ochre pastures and fresh air perfumed with heather, gorse and hay. Around its indented shores there was the addition of salty air laced with the aroma of seaweed thrown in by the raging oceans that surround the mystical isle. In the great emptiness only seagulls, puffins, cattle and sheep claimed ownership of the land. All this because most of its population had departed – emigrated to distant lands. The Ireland we used to know was indeed 'for the birds'.

The Atlantic continues to pound the western seaboard of the island, while Saint George's Channel to the south and the Irish Sea to the east are equally capable of unleashing violent storms at any time. Ireland, according to St Patrick, is water-bound and will end its days beneath the waves. Now, we islanders never took what he said quite literally but nevertheless treated his comment with respect. Of course, we don't know if the term 'beneath' refers to melting ice caps or whether his 'waves' were those of financial debt – or was he just jesting?

The limited fuel capacity of aircraft on transatlantic flights came as a windfall to the island, as Shannon in the south-west of Ireland became the recognised refuelling point for Europe. This new-found advantage for the region resulted in the establishing of the Shannon industrial estate and the duty-free airport, inspired by the late entrepreneur Brendan O'Regan. This was matched by the hydroelectric dam project created by Sean Lemass, who was then Taoiseach. A new direction had been found. But this was only the beginning of a hard-uphill battle to give the Republic new economic growth, which would eventually lead to joining the European Community, followed by a limited period of prosperity.

Memories of those times flash on the mind like a flickering black-and-white movie. One memory is that Gaelic games, along with golf, were almost the only sporting activities known in those days. People would laugh or show no interest if one suggested introducing a foreign sport, especially if it was associated with tropical climates!

Therefore, let us select surfing as a subject, and peer back over the years to see where it all began...

It was first sighted by westerners in the Hawaiian Islands in 1778 when it was chronicled by James King, a lieutenant serving with Captain James Cook's famous expedition to the Pacific. Cook was killed by natives in Kealakekua Bay, but King nevertheless wrote a description of the natives' ability to surf: 'When there is a great swell breaking on the reefs or the shore, twenty or thirty men and women go out on planks of about their own size. They select the biggest swell and push forward with their arms so as to stay on top and ride it to shore.' He observed the chiefs, known as Ali'i, used longer boards of from twelve to twenty-four feet to ride waves on beaches and the reefs specially selected for them alone.

History tells us that it was the Marquesas and the Polynesian people from Tahiti who originally discovered the Hawaiian Islands. The Polynesians were profound lovers of the ocean and the waves, and used short wooden boards just long enough to lie on which were called paipos. Today they are still used, but called body, skim or belly-boards. It was in the Hawaiian Islands that the really attractive art of standing upright on a board was perfected. As more and more foreigners and missionaries came to the islands, surfing declined.

Amazingly it was a young man called George Freeth, born in Ireland in 1883, who revived the sport. His parents immigrated to Oahu when he was an infant, and while still a young man he became so proficient in the sea that the example of his surfing encouraged others to imitate him. In 1907 the same young George Freeth was brought to Redondo Beach, California, where he demonstrated the sport and caught the imagination of the public.

One heroic event received wide publicity. It seems that in a storm George, entirely on his own, swam out and rescued six Japanese fishermen from a capsized boat, one by one. He was quite rightly awarded the Life Saving Corps medal of valour for his bravery. Sadly, due to his continual exposure to cold water, and because of a global flu epidemic, he died on 7th April 1919, at the early age of thirty-five.

It was therefore quite befitting that fifty-seven years later this spirit of Aloha would take root and grow, to embrace the youth in Ireland – the land of his heritage. And why not? Ireland has a maritime coast and an ocean equally as exciting as the Pacific – even if it is just a little cooler. The story of that flourishing is the one I want to tell in this book.

First a few basics. Although today the term 'surfing' is often associated with the World Wide Web, when related to the sea it becomes the sport of surfboard riding. This is where, as King recorded, one paddles out to sea on a board and rides a wave to shore, usually in a standing position. Over the years boards have evolved. In the beginning, they were made of wood but in the aftermath of World War II became modernised, having an interior of Styrofoam and an exterior coat of fibreglass. So as to attain direction and manoeuvrability a fin is fitted to the rear, while in more recently times epoxy resin is used for strength. All this development has enabled surfers to become more proficient at the sport while also giving them a wider selection of board sizes and shapes for their 'quiver'.

The waves, on the other hand, have been unchanged over the centuries, still being generated by distant storms or depressions. When they arrive, the local conditions determine how they will form. If the weather is calm and gentle the waves will break in harmony with the contours that lie beneath and thus be quite rideable, but if blown by local winds the waves will become distorted and more difficult to encounter.

In recent years mechanically propelled surfing has emerged as an extreme version of the sport. This is where the rider is brought like a water-skier on to the face of a wave that would normally be too large for paddling. They then let go of the tow rope and speed under the curl. This is a sophisticated form of surfing that relies on immense tropical storms or earthquakes to generate the large waves suited to the purpose.

Today surfboard riding in all forms attracts millions of people because of its many benefits: it's simple, it keeps one fit, and its costs are low once the initial equipment has been purchased, borrowed or rented. Surfing is also considered to be quite macho because of the way it has been portrayed by the movie industry – sunshine, sand and youthful adventure. Yet from another perspective something seems to attract from within: a struggle with the forces of nature.

Here we come face to face with what lies beneath. Physicists state that all moving objects have energy due to their motion, and this is called kinetic energy. This energy is found locked inside swell – as that is what makes waves in the first place. The surfrider also possesses kinetic energy which is released by paddling fast. As the wave approaches the energy is still contained inside its mass. As the surfer pivots on top of the wave there is a release of potential energy, and then in the drop all this energy escapes in the form of an exploding wave and a thirty-mile-per-hour surfer heading shoreward. Physics is sport in action!

Other invisible forces are released in the form of electromagnetic waves which travel at the speed of light. All this is coupled with and drawn down by gravitation, something of which one is all too aware! To sum up, the surfer has experienced three segments of kinetic energy and two forms of the forces of nature – electromagnetic and gravitational. This cocktail underlies the vision of a great wave and a fleeting surf rider; beneath the beauty the elements are locked in combat with chaos, and cushioned with pure H_2O, while the rider must at all times maintain the dynamic balance of a ballerina. Call that a simple sport?

CHAPTER 1

Here and Now

Time flows ever so fast, and already it is 'now' and in a small bay in County Sligo an aged surfer – myself, Kevin Cavey – lying on my surfboard and wearing a winter wetsuit, battle my way out through the ocean in pursuit of my friends. Surfing has been a constant in my life. It is always a wonderful experience, even though these days I find it more difficult to perform. At the same time, I am glad to have kept in touch with the sport. At the very least I can still catch a ride, though it will not be overly impressive to spectators – but more important, I am still in touch with my surfing friends and they in turn keep me applied, God bless them.

The waves today have five- to seven-foot faces – challenging and suitable for my more youthful friends such as Tim, who is a spectacular surfer and no less, Fergus, Mike, Ciaran, Kieran, Rob, John, Conor, Simon, Lisa, Jens, Charlotte, Phil, Kenny, Sophie, Fergus, Chris, Gerard, Simon and many of whom are here and taking magnificent rides as usual.

It is not by chance that the group are here today but because they have studied the wave and wind forecast on Magic Seaweed and perhaps Wind Guru. The days of looking at the sky or asking a fisherman to forecast have gone. Today it is a measured exercise. As I near the group, someone paddles his long board down the front of a wobbling wave curling to his right. This is a big one, and with aggression and poise he cranks a bottom turn. A moment later, the wave encases him in a cylinder of spewing liquid – he has caught a barrel. Moments later he rises to the top of the crest and cuts over the back, now ready for his next surfing opportunity. On the other side of the bay there is Barry riding another long board with distinction, while others – John, Neil and Eoin – are riding short boards on similar waves that break from the opposite direction. These acrobats are exploding their energies down steep sections, while at the same time whipping their boards over the unfortunate waves. Yes, this is how advanced surfing has become.

Suddenly my thoughts are interrupted. Instinctively I turn my board and paddle before a five-foot wall of Atlantic splendour. Six strokes and I am flying downwards and to my left while crouching with the sun reflecting in my eyes. Though I cannot see properly, I know I have caught the wave, because of the jerk as my board hits the trough and streaks across the peeling face. Phew, that's great, this time I have made it, and that does not always happen. I take two more rides, not quite as good as the first, but that is always that way. Already, it is time to retire before my friends come in beaming with joy and recounting their performances in detail.

Today, I think to myself, though the waves are busy with very advanced surfers, the scene remains the same – wetsuits, boards, cold water and plenty of banter. There are some fourteen clubs around the country all linked to one Irish Association. There have also been massive technical advances with sophisticated boards and equipment, but the real difference is the people. Surfers are now in such abundance it is often difficult to find a wave that does not have several other people trying to catch it. Because of numbers, people no longer wave to each other on the highways and generally act quite aloof. Very many do not join clubs but just hang out with their immediate friends and look for waves to suit their level, and much of this happens with limited social interaction. Then, as with the Hawaiian Ali'i, there is a tendency for locals to have secret places to call their own, a place where the waves will not become crowded. It happened over three hundred years ago, why not once again?

Most of this is the antithesis of what surfing in Ireland originally stood for. In the beginning, it was almost like an apostolic message being delivered. Everyone was told about the sport and conversation brought about networking and great contacts. Everyone knew someone who was interested and those links were followed up. However, times change and so must we. Though unrecognisable in black suits and hoods, many of the new surfing breed who paddle out or whizz down the highways are the grandchildren of that original brigade who surfed Ireland's first green waves many years ago.

Just then I heard the quark of a seagull and the sound of someone letting out a triumphant cry. Then in a flash my mind stretches into the past and I remember the shouts from the old brigade: Roger, Pat, Harry, Hughie, Brian, Vivienne, Tom, Jane, Dave, Mike, Camel, Tony, Davy, Alan, Bo, Charlie, Dermot, Sam, Roci, Declan, Ger and so on. These were some of the original adventurers who first pioneered the sport on our emerald shores. They would not have worn cosy neoprene wetsuits or used perfumed 'sex wax', as it is called. They would have used battered ten-foot boards rubbed with candle wax to stop slipping and worn leaky diver's suits with holes. What's more, they would only have arrived at the beach on the off chance and mainly for the fun. Yes, these veterans would be surfing for all the wrong reasons except one: they loved the sport.

Origins

The Irish enchantment with the sea was first noted in 1874 when John Philip Holland from Liscannor, Co. Clare, then living in America, submitted his plan to the secretary of the US Navy for a submarine. Perhaps it was from living originally in Co. Clare where many surfers would later emerge, or perhaps it was the Viking gene resurfacing, but either way it was the first successful attempt of its sort.

Let's lift the Celtic veil and peer back again at that time well before the 'big bang' or the 'first three minutes' of Irish surfing began, to a time when most of the future's known surfers were not even born. It was 1949 and a film called Thrill of the Surf was launched, showing board building and surf rescue. The narrator insisted that surfing was Australia's number one national sport, with the result that the public came to agree. Soon Movietone News showed repeated footage of people riding immensely long boards in Waikiki, some wearing hats and sunglasses, and one even had a pet dog riding on the nose of a board.

This of course had its effect in Ireland where many young people with astute eyes for adventure were looking on. Quite unobserved, there was a change in the depth of the Irish soul where its teenagers had new ideas and ambitions about how to improve their lot. Some free spirits had designs and dreams of their own, and were quite willing to experiment with an almost unknown sport called surfing.

In the early 1900s folklore tells us that there was an unknown woman in Kerry who was riding waves. She has never been identified but is alleged to have surfed in Ballyheigue. If this is true then it was likely that she used a bodyboard, as standing was only for those who could afford glossy magazines or visit the cinema, where she might have seen a film made in 1895, La Mer, that depicts the small broken waves of the sea into which bathers are running and jumping. She might also have seen The Popular Sport of Surf Boarding made in Australia in 1925. This film showed boardriders at North Bondi, manoeuvring their boards into position, catching the breaks and the standing up. How could she resist the temptation to emulate?

At the same time, in Britain the sport of belly-boarding had become well known and quite a part of the holiday norm. Surf bathing, as it was called, grew in popularity as seaside holidays became more available and affordable. An early photo of a man with a surfboard was taken on a Cornish beach and dated 1904. It is also said that in 1910 a London newspaper had a surfing illustration on its front page. There was a female surfer called Jenny Rilstone who was to remain a surfer all her life. There were two soldiers, George Tamlyn and William Saunders, who returned from the First World War where they had been in contact with South Africans who in turn had told them all about belly-boarding. However, up till then all of this surfing activity was done on wooden bodyboards also known as paipos. This changed for the better and surfing got good press, when in 1920, Prince Edward was photographed taking stand-up surfing lessons from Duke Kahanamoku in Waikiki.

Joe Roddy

In 1949, one person took a creative and alternative view of the world around him. He was impressed by what was happening in the world of aquatics. Joe Roddy, the son of a Dundalk lighthouse keeper, was about to launch his very own secret weapon. He was just fourteen at the time, a strong young fellow of about 5 feet 8 inches in height, bearing a mop of brown hair and a broad grin. This lad was an adventurer and a romantic at heart, as he also possessed the talent of being a first-class dancer, much to the admiration of the lassies around Dundalk. He loved the sea and experimented with designs for undersea diving equipment made from whatever he could muster. However, more important was that secret weapon.

Joe had been doing some reading and was inspired to build a four-meter Lifeguard-style surfboard. To do this he said that he used tea chests and lighthouse paint. The sleek craft once completed was used as a boat which could be propelled by using a paddle. More interestingly, however, he used it to paddle the waves that drifted into his secluded bay. One day he got the attention of the swimmers on the beach, who marvelled at his expertise, and word spread around the locality. Joe said that he introduced some kids to paddling his board, but the sport didn't take off at the time. It was just after World War II and food was in short supply; there was a shortage of money and very little transport or communication. He thought little about his achievement and moved to greener pastures such as, building a sailing boat. From then on, he devoted the rest of his life to the ocean. He eventually took over his father's business, running boat trips from Valentia to the Skelligs – a life on the ocean blue.

One of the fathers of Irish surfing, Hugh O'Brien-Moran of Tramore, describes Joe's return to the sport many years later:

'On Saturday, 20th June 2009 Joe went out for a midsummer surf. The surf was small but well-shaped. Half a dozen of us went out with Joe including stand-up paddleboarder Jim Swift. I had a camera and was trying to figure out a way to get a photograph without pressurising Joe to go beyond his comfort zone. He hadn't been on a board for fifty-seven years, so the possibility was that he might be a bit rusty. I needn't have worried. First, he stood on the board in shallow water, then left the paddle behind and took a few waves lying prone. Finally, he took a few waves standing up using the paddle. We were cheering, moved by the fact that we were witnessing him spanning sixty years of surfing on that day. Joe rode the wave with a relaxed stance, knees slightly bent, with the youthful look of a natural athlete. At the same time, he had a proud and noble bearing that comes with age. There was no trace of tension that would lead you to believe that he lacked confidence in his own ability. He was stoked after the session, and so were we. He is involved in boats and he spoke in nautical terms about the board – something like when he "leaned on the stern the bow came around". He was using a paddle, which I understand was the way he originally surfed. We were all concerned for his safety, considering his age. To keep fit he competes successfully in ballroom dancing contests, and gave us a demonstration at our T Bay Surf Club Legends' Ball.'

Joe Roddy with replica of his original board built in 1946

Spreading the Word

In 1949 even in California, surfing was still in its infancy, and that same year a young and enthusiastic Greg Noll was only learning to surf at his local 'El Porto' on a cumbersome redwood board he had made himself. In his own words Greg recalled, 'It's amazing how long it took to get to the point where you could stand up on those boards. I just rode the soup in those early years.' Despite his early beginnings Greg was to become one of the world's biggest big-wave riders, mainly in Waimea on the Hawaiian island of Oahu. Yes, every success story is analogous to a house that looks so attractive, yet no one gives a thought to the painful hours that went into building it, brick by brick; surfing in Ireland would be no exception.

In that same ominous year, I was just seven, and living in County Dublin but also felt the pangs, the threads, of a hazy ambition. My call to the sea came about in a roundabout way. I was fascinated by the stories told about World War II. It seemed to me as if I had lived before and in another life, somewhere where the sun shone hot and the folk were friendly and Spanish moss hung from the trees. This somewhere could have been Mississippi, South Carolina or God knows where. Maybe I was influenced by the fact that one of my grandmothers was from Ohio or that my Belfast mother adored American history. However, one day I spied a story in the newspaper that was lying on the kitchen table. It showed a picture of many battleships in flames. I asked my Dad what it was all about. He looked at the newspaper and responded,

'Well, Kevin, that was on December 7th, 1941, when the Japanese attacked Pearl Harbour and sank half of the US Pacific fleet!'

I recoiled in shock as I had never realised that a power like the United States, where cowboys roamed and Gene Kelly sang in the rain, could be so badly caught. This was preposterous, but nevertheless it represented more attraction to the Pacific. I began to read about how the Higgins landing craft was perfected in the southern swamps of Louisiana and the development of amphibious warfare. But more importantly, I learned about, Oahu, where tough guys rode waves on huge wooden boards and where the great George Freeth and Duke Kahanamoku pioneered paddled on to swells of enormous heights. This whole package, set in the Hawaiian archipelago along with its haunting music, was the nirvana of my imagination. It was somewhere here that the sea part got predominance with life shaping results. My Dad had a keen eye for a bargain and in the late Forties noticed a thirty-bedroom hotel for sale in Bray, which lies just south of Dublin. Having the Midas touch was quite natural for him, as his brother was the Irish distributor of Jaguar cars and his uncle had introduced Quaker Oats to Ireland, so why not Bill? He developed the Royal Hotel over the following twenty years to become a Grade A-star property with a hundred and thirty rooms, bars, restaurants and facilities for functions. Thus, I was destined to become both a hotelier and a lifetime surfer.

Rossnowlagh

About the same time another hotel-minded man was busy developing his new purchase. This was in Rossnowlagh in Co. Donegal. It was to be called the Sandhouse Hotel, due to its being situated directly upon a magnificent stretch of beach that was constantly blessed with beautiful waves. Vinnie Britton, the owner, was not only a businessman but he also physically built his own extensions. His four-star hotel still overlooks Rossnowlagh beach on Donegal Bay. It eventually offered a luxury spa, Jacuzzi, an award-winning restaurant and free parking. The sixty spacious rooms at the hotel all feature bathrooms and showers, and many rooms have panoramic sea views. Vinnie himself was often to be found with his close friends enjoying a neat whiskey and whiling the time away in his one and only Boss's Bar, not to be confused with the Surfers Bar that was to become the home of an archive of memorabilia of the sport. Because of Mary Britton's appreciation of the best things in life, she filled the hotel with antiques and period furniture and developed the habit of having a log fire in the front hall. The hotel is also enhanced by the skill of a very good chef. My parents had stayed in the Sandhouse and knew the Brittons personally. It wasn't long before this hotel and the Britton family would later be instrumental in the development of surfing in Ireland.

Mary Britton had gone to school with a young girl from Galway who married a Galway man by the name of Naughton. In 1950, they decided that as nothing was happening in Ireland they would immigrate to the east coast of the United States. It was there that they had a son called Kevin. When young Kevin Naughton was seven they moved to Huntington Beach in California, the very place where George Freeth had been a lifeguard and surfer in years gone by. Now the stage was set for something large in the world of

Irish/American surfing to occur. This would just take a few more years to unfold.

Five years after the Naughtons emigrated, a young male visitor called Ian Hill began to surf, and dream about the Donegal coast. Though it was only 1955, the history and imagery of surfing had already had an impact on him. Ian was from Southport in the north-west of England and had become an ardent belly-boarder. All this activity in the sea rather added to his fitness. It also contributed to his gaining entry to the Royal Air Force, where he became a physical fitness instructor. He knew all about the surfing of the time, about its development in Cornwall and Devon and also about big-wave riding in the Pacific. He had never been to Ireland but hoped to go there some day; the endless miles of Atlantic seaboard coastline appealed to his romantic imagination.

County Wicklow

Meantime, I had reached the age of thirteen. Much to my surprise my parents sold up in Rathmines and moved to live in Bray. However, there were immediate compensations. One was that I had a great school friend who shared the bus to and from school. This was Jurek Delimata, who was of Polish descent. Jurek was very scientific-minded and loved all manner of conversations about outer space and the BBC's That Was the Week that Was. I began to use my binoculars to gaze at the moon at night and was thrilled to get a clear view of craters. Encounters with Jurek were hilarious and laughter became our middle name. Secondly there was a great winter storm that hit Bray and flooded the seafront; and what's more it washed away the lighthouse at the end of the harbour. I found this very exciting, but I also noted how big the sea could be in an east coast storm. Thirdly, as the summer came, an olive-green-coloured amphibious vehicle arrived on the beach. It was called a DUKW, pronounced as 'duck' and a left-over from World War II. This six-wheeled boat-cum-truck could go on land or sea and reminded me of my wartime fantasies. Of course, it was soon over-painted in yellow for the sake of tourism.

Another bonus was the rediscovery of a swimming spot in Naylor's Cove, a north-east facing inlet at the base of Bray Head. That direction in the Irish Sea is usually bad business, and because of heavy north-east winds eventually caused is eventual demise. In its halcyon years, it consisted of a series of three outdoor swimming pools which were created by the simple construction of a heavy sea wall. This was the home of the Bray Cove Swimming Club where the countless swimming galas were held. This was where I taught finally myself to swim. Later the icing on the cake came when my folks brought me to visit Brittas Bay in County Wicklow where I discovered miles of sand dunes, and it seemed warmer than most other places. The only inhabitants of this forgotten corner were curlews, seagulls and a very few people. This was a dream come true and all less than an hour from home. To add to the enjoyment there were sometimes some small waves. Therefore, I bought a skim board with the turned-up front and began to use it while propelled with swim fins to catch waves galore. Then there was a cove adjacent to Brittas, and it was called Magheramore. Later this was to become recognised as the best surfing spot on Ireland's east coast, but more about this later.

Snowboarders

In 1959, a new surfing movie was released by Columbia Pictures and featured Sandra Dee as Gidget, a girl with a passion to surf. The film depicted southern California, where surfing was at the time, and became the driving force and focus of a youthful craze to surf at all costs. It was an all-time hit (though quite silly when viewed in later years). Now Ireland was a far cry from Sunny California and dull-to-freezing weather was the norm, but there was always an Irish answer to an Irish problem. In the winter of that year the snow had been falling for a couple of days. My school pal Jurek and I decided to go to the Sugar Loaf mountain in Co.

Wicklow to sleigh ride. Jurek was great company, full of literary flare laced with good humour and a vivid imagination. Just to be different, we had perfected a method of standing upright on the sleigh while holding a rope tied to the front. However, all this had prompted something else to happen. In a flash of genius Jurek said,

'Why not use your skimboard?'

I answered with a grunt and said, 'Our feet will slip off.'

But that evening we became absorbed in an experiment extraordinaire. We took the skim board and, using Evo-Stick, glued two of my Dad's galoshes to the deck. Now all we would have to do was slip our feet into the galoshes and ride down the hill standing.

'Crazy, but what'll stop us falling over?'

'Cricket stumps of course,' Jurek replied.

Next day, armed with the shoe-glued surfboard, we climbed into my Dad's car and drove up the long hill to the Sugar Loaf. By then the snowfall had abated and the sun was shining. It was pretty cold and in those days winter gear was scarce and so we clad in anything we could find: jumpers, anoraks, two pairs of pants each, and wool gloves that froze the fingers. The snowy field sloped downwards for about a thousand yards. It looked inviting, and as luck had it there were almost no spectators. I dug my shoes into the rubber galoshes and with a push from the stumps, began a speedy traverse to the left, followed by a swing to the right using a cricket stump to pivot.

'Whee, it works!' I shouted, gliding ever downwards.

That day we took turns, happy in the knowledge of what we had achieved, but unaware that we had 'invented' something as valuable as plastic.

During that same year, however, a young man up in Fehan near Buncranna, Co. Donegal was using skim boards as they should be used! Eddie Stewart, who lived later in both Dublin and Lahinch, reported:

'Our first boards (which we still use) were bought from a sports shop in Derry run by Tommy Orr. He received a small consignment of boards in 1956. He was not quite sure what they were (he was a very high-powered cricketer) but my father knew and bought five. They are made of five-ply marine plywood, and measure four foot by one foot, slightly bent up at the front and rounded. These are bodyboards – not long nor buoyant enough for standing up. You just catch the wave on the break and get pushed in. Grazed knees were always a sign of good surf. We rode at Tullagh Bay, just west of Malin Head, near Clonmany. There were other shores nearby, but with dangerous undertows. Also, we featured at Culdaff just east of Malin Head, when conditions permitted, and Ballymastocker near Portsalon on other occasions.'

CHAPTER 2

Touching the Monolith

It was late August of that same year, 1962, when the phone rang at our home. It was my friend and buddy, Paddy Carroll. At the time Paddy was studying to become a Holy Ghost father. His Dad was a chief superintendent in the police and he was also on the Irish Olympic Council. They had a house in Waterville, Co. Kerry, and I was invited to join them for a week in the summer. The house was one of a terrace that had been built for the workers on the transatlantic cable that provided the phone link between the USA and Europe.

Waterville in those days was the favourite vacation spot for Charlie Chaplin. It was easy to understand why he visited so often; the area, true to its soft-sounding name, was equally soft on the eye. It was surrounded by magnificent high mountains that seemed always to be capped with mist. Ballinskelligs Bay, as it was called, was long, curved and open to the Atlantic, though the beach was spotted with rocks. One evening after a farmhouse-style meal of ham and salad with loads of brown bread and gallons of tea, we settled down beside the turf fire. Paddy was engrossed in a novel. I had just finished reading a Korean War book set in 1950 in which the Marines had made a fighting retreat from the Chosun reservoir. Mella, Paddy's sister, who was also enjoying a novel, yawned, looked up and said,

'What are you reading, Kev?'

So, I held up my book for all to see.

She looked at the front cover and said,

'How can you read such awful stuff? Look, it's all blood and guts.'

My heart missed a beat. I had never thought about it that way before; killing was just Hollywood stuff, it didn't happen much in real life. Also, I was only interested in the logistics and strategies used. Now I felt like a dope, and tried to cover up with a laugh while reaching for the nearest magazine available. So, I picked up a copy of the Reader's Digest.

'Look now, I'm reading excellent quality material,' I said with a chuckle. Then I flicked the Digest open, and there right before my eyes was a picture of a native surfing a head-high wave in the Hawaiian Islands! To my amazement, the wave was no bigger than I had often seen in Kerry. In a flash, the synapses fired and the neurons went into overdrive, making the connection between my aquatic past and probable future. A picture of a wind-blown wave loomed in my mind. It was breaking on one of Ireland's long golden beaches, and there was a person riding it, and that person was me! I would be as free as a bird, and a spectacle of amazement to those who witnessed. I was going to be a surfer, and put Ireland on the map!

I turned with new-found zeal and triumphantly blurted, 'Paddy – that's what I'm going to do from now on,' pointing at the illustration.

They looked at me in with pity, as I passed the Digest for all to read.

First Stand-up Boards

As far as I could see, there was no one stand up surfing in Ireland yet. The time had come to move up a notch and hurry along with the full-size surfboard. This move was necessary if I were to get properly into the sport. I therefore purchased a sheet of eight-foot by four-foot marine plywood and hauled it to the basement of the family home and commenced work. This was to become the first of two experimental boards. I had saved an article in a magazine about Joel de Rosney and George Hennebutte in Biarritz. The story told about his big-wave riding and his band of surfing compatriots, Michel Barland and Jacky Rott, who began to make the first French fibreglass surfboards. As luck had it, there were plenty of pictures of boards, though as they were in the water I did not notice they had a fin. Bearing all this in mind I tapered it narrow at one end and rounded it at the nose and coated it with marine varnish. Perhaps this is excusable, as many of the older pictures of Hawaiian surfers were with boards that had no fins. The next challenge was to make it buoyant. Ideally a board should be built like a thin boat – with ribs, and hollow in the centre. However, that would have been too expensive and way too difficult, so I took a short cut. I bought sheets of Styrofoam and stuck them in layers to the underside. In turn, the Styrofoam was also coated in endless layers of marine varnish till it was quite tough and waterproof. Lastly, I took a candle, lit it and let it drop spots all over the deck. This was to stop my feet slipping off.

My second experimental Styrofoam and Marine Plywood
Surfboard – now housed in the T Bay Surfing Centre in Tramore.

Had I realised it, but up North Desmond Vance, known as 'Bo', was also wondering about building a surfboard. He intended doing it the conventional way using Styrofoam as a base and fibreglass for the surface. This was not going to be an easy undertaking and he was not yet sure if surfing would work in Ireland.

On the evening before launching my board I checked the weather reports for the east coast area. This involved phoning the weather bureau and asking the wind direction and speed for the east coast and Bray area. In those times, they were pleased to discuss the subject and were therefore very helpful. From what they said, tomorrow was to be the day. I reckoned on that occasion the centre of Bray seafront opposite the bandstand would be best place to launch. I wanted an onshore wind because the Irish Sea does not receive long-distance swells like in the west. I selected a time when it would be a half tide, not too deep or too low, as I had noticed that when the tide is low, the waves get smaller and also crash hard, when it is too high, it becomes too deep for the waves to break, though they are usually much bigger at that stage.

In the late summer of 1962, with the help of my brother, I placed my coffin-shaped surfboard ceremoniously on top of my mother's Ford Anglia car and used cushions and rope, as a roof rack. The wind had been blowing from the night before, but now it was accompanied by rain. Then I headed for the beach, carefully avoiding the route that past the family hotel. The waves were breaking some fifty yards from shore and were about waist high. This was not great but it would do. A man stopped to watch me carry the board to the water's edge. He said, as most do,

'You must be mad getting in on a day like this!'

It was still summer; why would a geek be so dim? I thought as I grinned back like a chimp caught in the pantry. I heard Colm chuckle at my plight. Then with a smile I launched the board, lay on it, and began to paddle out, already delighted because I found it was quite buoyant. I ploughed through the oncoming walls of water and finally got outside beyond the break. I was now alone in the midst of moving green peaks and an even greener Bray Head looming to my right.

I saw some large waves approaching, turned the board towards shore and began to paddle very hard. Then like a cannon shot, I was pitched forward as the wave pushed me along. In an instant, I jumped to my feet letting out a shout of joy. I glided towards shore in a buzz of excitement. I was now standing on a surfboard, on a wave, and travelling straight toward the beach. It had not entered my head that soon I would want to turn and manoeuvre, but of course this could not be done without a fin! There could be no celebration of the event because there were no other surfers. This gave me food for thought: I would also have to form a club!

In the meantime, back on the beach, my younger brother began to take note of the happenings but he had a different perspective of events. He was amused to see his older brother act like a kid. Years later, when asked to describe early surfing, Colm elaborated:

'I only used my brother's boards but not his very first one that was launched in Bray, because I thought it was a liability. His very first was a homemade board made with a sheet of plywood with about three or four sheets of aero board stuck in layers to give it buoyancy. It was huge and very heavy. I could only describe it as trying to surf on a giant omelette. It sat on the water like it was dead. Its weight prevented it from bobbing up and down on the waves. It just sat there and the waves went through it. When he next went out on it, all I saw was him standing briefly before tipping over like a comedian. However, I reckoned it all looked like a bit of fun, and I might get to meet some girls if I tagged along!'

Following that one day in 1962 while on a wave hunt with Colm we went to Magheramore. He said that he knew a fellow called Aidan Cummins with a house on the cliffs overlooking the bay. True enough there above a picturesque cove with waves, was Aidan in his parent's summer house or shack as it turned out to be. With a whoop! I unloaded the new board and carefully carried it down the cliff path. There were swimmers that day and one of them was Simon Digby whose parents owned a very nice summer home on the laneway leading to the beach. However, there was also rather unfit looking man entering the water and starting to swim out through the waves. I noted that he had chosen the place where a small stream hits the sea and causes a small rip. He was therefore able to glide out through the waves that were about four feet and normally too big for one of his ability. A moment later, he was calling for help. My second try out on the new plank was now going to be an attempted rescue! Getting him in was not too difficult as he just hung on the back of the board while I paddled him to safety. Just as we reached the shore a large set of waves hit us and sheared off most of the Styrofoam under the deck. He buzzed off and left me staring with despair at the beach littered with broken Styrofoam pieces. Aidan and Colm both looked on laughing at the comic event. Since then coastal erosion has undermined the shack with no trace of its prior existence. Simon who was the swimmer then began to get into surfing, and built a wooden board as part of a school project. The Digby's still (in 2017) use the summer house and their families surf in Magheraghmore every summer.

At the same time in Rossnowlagh, Mary and Vinnie Britton of the Sandhouse Hotel had been blessed with five young boys: Brian, Conor, Barry, William and David. The eldest, Brian, was a studious fellow, who at that stage took the sea for granted as he had not yet grasped its enormous potential. However, just four years later all that was to change. In the meantime, Vinnie continued to improve his property by adding rooms, function facilities and a marine-style bar with a beach entrance. Meanwhile a young Aer Lingus pilot from Clontarf named Johnny was touring the area, and when he got to Bundoran admired the waves and wondered if anyone could surf them. Johnny would soon become one of the sport's pioneers.

In Belfast, the young and progressive Bo Vance was now using a body board on the north shore, and pondering how to make a fullsized board and wondering if anyone else was interested! In Dunmore East, Eddie Stewart was still involved in the sport, and said later that when holidaying at Renvyle in 1962 they discovered Carrowniskey, now one of Mayo's best surfing areas. His Dad had an original board with a turned-up front and his sisters subsequently had an unusual body board called Kon-Tiki, made of balsa, which was good for lighter people. She must have been one of the early 'wahines' of Irish surfing. Eddie used long boards in later years when he visited Australia, but now back in Ireland he still uses plywood body boards with turned-up fronts all shaped and copied from his Dad's original purchase.

Ian Hill

In 1962, up north there was another young person already very interested in surfing. It was the aforementioned Ian Hill, who by now had finished his time in the air force and had joined the British Customs and Excise department. As fate would have it, he was posted to Derry in Northern Ireland and this put him fairly and squarely within striking distance of some of the best surfing beaches on the island. Just like the lad, he was armed with his paipo belly-board and a pair of diver's fins (flippers), but with the addition of an old van he began to travel around the north-west looking for good wave breaks. Ian says that he even made it as far south as Spanish Point in Co. Clare. His long years in the service were now paying off – in his strength, stamina and determination. He loved his newfound life on this rugged island standing like a bulwark to the Atlantic Ocean, being fed green energy with the compliments of Mother Nature. Ian was also to have a surfing visitor from California. It was Miki Dora, otherwise known as 'Da Cat', here from his native Malibu. He had decided to spend time in Ireland and headed north-west, ending up in Enniscrone. He stayed there for a while and later said how much he enjoyed the quality of the surf in amazing bay. He also grumbled at length about the cold and sometimes sheer misery that accompanied that experience. Sometime after that, on the recommendation of his ex-girlfriend Linda C, he went to Portrush, where he met Ian. When he returned to California, he said he could not understand why anyone surfed in the Irish climate. However, he had one bad habit that I hope he did not pick up in Ireland. Miki used to swing and dance his board around, thus driving the other surfers off his waves, particularly in Malibu where he was king.

Talk of a club and Ardmore Studios

It was September of 1963, and I was now working for my Dad in his hotel. After being in America it took me months to properly settle back into living and working in the real world. Our real world was quite unreal because many of our clientele were from the Ardmore film studios. There were stars coming and going and amongst these were Catherine Hepburn, Lawrence Harvey, Aldo Ray, Peggy Cummins, Terrence Morgan, Sarah Miles and Kevin Mc Clory the director of James Bond movies. The celebrity film star Peter O'Toole was staying in the hotel while filming 'The Lion in the winter'. One of his wishes was that his bedroom be stocked with Disc Bleu, French cigarettes. I understood his passion because these were also my favourites. He always drank in the hotel bar after work. One night there was a difficulty over this! As management, we were at fault because we did not inform him that the bar was to be renovated. When he arrived as usual about 8pm, to his dismay, the Bar was closed and cleared of stock. He called for the duty manager who was unfortunately myself. I apologised for not informing him and offered an alternative place in the hotel for him to socialise. He became perplexed and demanded that the bar be opened as usual. I showed him that the whole area had been cleared and could not be re-instated. At this point, someone caught me by the throat and banged my head against a picture the wall. Ironically it was a picture of Wally Forsyth Surfing Sunset Point Break! This 18 x 24-inch picture took the brunt of my head, smashing the glass. The standoff lasted perhaps a minute and concluded when his assistant pulled the assailant away. The group immediately checked out of the hotel, thus leaving us short of an important VIP. Soon after that the story goes that he and a friend bought a pub of their own called The Hole in the Wall so they could drink as late as they wished from then on.

In June 1963, I got to work on my second stand-up board, but of far more importance, the country went into a state of excitement as President J.F. Kennedy visited Ireland and both Jurek and I got to see him in O'Connel Street.

The story went like this. Jurek was employed in Aer Lingus sales, and their office was on the second floor overlooking the west end of Dublin's O'Connel Street. He invited me to come and see the cavalcade driving from Parnell Square. As I arrived early we got bored and made paper darts and fired them out at the onlookers below. This was a harmless prank but just then the cavalcade arrived and to our horror one of the darts sped towards President Kennedy's open car. We gasped and held our breaths but is hit the ground just ahead of the car and was run over. Those were innocent times. As he passed beneath the window we got a face on view of him in his medium blue suit, sandy hair and sallow skin. Then he was gone, just a memory.

Putting that aside and almost as important to some, I got to see a movie called 'Ride the Wild Surf' with Tab Hunter in the lead – but never in the surf, as the surf guru, Phil Edwards doubled for him. Though I was feeling dispirited with my surfing progress to date, the film helped spur my determination and I got busy getting a few skimboarding friends together and telling them they were now members of Ireland's first surf club. I reckoned it was about time we had a letterhead and envelope to make a statement about the club-to-be. I labelled it 'Bray Ireland Surf Club' just so it would be easily identified by people at home and abroad.

All this meant that I had to work hard assembling a balsa board kit that I had now purchased. When working on the board in our basement of my folk's house, and to be 'in the groove' I wore a floral shirt and smoked a corn cob, while playing endless Hawaiian music. I possessed cherry blend tobacco from the New World, and this aroma mixed with the stench of paint must have been an unhealthy concoction. Finished, the board was ten feet long and two feet wide, absolutely flat but had a rounded nose and tail. There was no fin, but the importance of this omission was not appreciated till later, when serious surfing began. Jurek advised that the shape should be more like a cigar or a teardrop. We settled for his suggestion and sheared some balsa from below the front and back to create a rocker or curve. I then lashed on yellow paint and finished the job with some white lines swishing fore and aft, Aloha style. This board later became bright red and was taken on our first Surfari.

I reckoned that to promote the sport, I needed a good camera. Father Patrick Carroll, told me of a seminarian who was selling a camera in Kimmage Manor College. It was a Pentax with removable 400mm lens, along with a tripod and some other odds and ends – for ir£40. It was a stiff price, but served the purpose. With it, I managed to take many of Ireland's first surfing pictures, though most of the shots were in small waves, and nothing like what Surfer Magazine of California produces. However, the shots did reflect the conditions and the people of the times. I began telling the magazine about our activity and sent them quite a few pictures. All this was to have a good result later.

Roci Allan,

It was still 1964 and in New York the Beatles, who were top of the UK charts, were interviewed on the Ed Sullivan show. They appeared for thirteen minutes, during which they sang five songs and caused a national sensation. In Vietnam an incident in the Gulf of Tonkin, that caused a significant increase of US forces. Back in the wee island, I broke up with my first real sweetheart, called Yvonne. Yes, it was very difficult and harder than all the penance that Lough Derg could provide! Lough Derg is a place of penance that only the Irish could think up. One stays up all night and prays and does this while fasting. It is a great character builder and good for the soul I'm told. I hope that's true because I have gone there many times over the years.

In the UK, Ian Hill, now made an historic trip from Derry to Bude in Cornwall, where he met Bill Bailey of Bilbo Surfboards. He immediately bought a board and returned to Ireland with this new gem. In the following months, he began to venture to the beaches that he already knew, but this time the difference was his standing erect while riding the waves to shore. The first such venture was during Easter at Castle Rock. On this first occasion, he surfed wearing only jeans and a T-shirt. He continued from then using the nearest beaches, Portrush and Portstewart, followed by an expedition to Donegal, Bundoran and Tullan Strand. Ian was now quite advanced in the sport, whereas as I still relied on my balsa plank.

Then a visitor, Ian Hill, surfing at Bundoran in 1964

At the same time as all this was happening a young Italian-looking guy from Enniskillen, who was appropriately named Roci Allan, was also delving into the mysteries of surfing. Roci tells his own story:

'In August 1964, my sister Susan and I had been lent a surfboard by a lady from England called Muriel Fawcett, who brought it

24

over from Cornwall to Rossnowlagh. Somewhere in the house I have a Polaroid of Sue and me on the boards, standing up on a nine-inch wave! I was completely into rugby at the time, playing for school, town and anybody who would have me, until in 1970 I sustained a bad knee injury playing against the army. After three weeks of hospital and surgery I was told never to play again and the following summer I looked for a new sport and remembered about surfing.'

'Although we lived in Enniskillen, every summer was spent in Rossnowlagh, and there my current girlfriend took me to see Davy Govan and Alan Duke surfing at Tullan (her best friend was Davy's girlfriend), just after the '71 Europeans. I asked around and found that two other Enniskillen lads, Dave Pierce and Grant Robinson, had just taken up the sport, so that winter I joined them in trips to the coast. My father, who was a doctor, was just glad to see I wasn't sliding back into rugby and risking a permanent disability.

Was I spoiled?

Just to mention that at 21, I was offered a sport car by my parents. However, I declined the kind offer because I did not want to look like a spoiled Kid. If I was to be spoiled - it was going to be in a different way! A year later my Dad fell ill and he could not go on a Hoteliers trip to the East coast of USA. He offered me his tickets which I graciously accepted. The trip started in Southampton where we boarded the Cunard's liner, Queen Elizabeth for a five-day journey to New York. This was the most fantastic gift I could imagine. It was amazing to watch the people coming on board at Southampton, one person was carrying a birdcage. I thought that this trip was way too good for me yet I made friends Swiss, English, Israeli, American and a Canadian. I also met a family from Clearwater near Tampa. They were the Oppel family of Italian Irish descent. They insisted that I come over to stay, when in Miami. Therefore, I rented a car, left the tour, and drove west. They lived at Sun heights, Lago with their back-yard opening into grapefruit groves. This was real America without pretence. A few days later Ann, Patty, Greg and Ray took me in their 57' Chevy to do the promised scuba diving at Crystal River, something that turned out to be a monumental experience. Firstly, the aluminium boat, engine and scuba equipment had to be secured. After thirty minutes travelling between palm laden islands, we arrived at the diving area. Suddenly the murky water turned crystal clear because we were at a spring delivering fresh water up from below. The dive was like descending in the Caribbean. The spring was like a conical crater with small fish circling in very bright light. All was well till at about twenty-five feet, I needed to clear my mask for the second time, but it did not work! Eeek! I panicked, and shot to the surface. The others in the boat looked with horror as my nose was pumping blood. I had been foolish. Once over that excitement, we landed on Banana Island and had a barbecue and watched the sun setting. That night we went to Pattie's college hop and heard Gene Pitney sing CC Ryder amongst other hits of the time. The in style for guys was candy striped, button down or snap shirts and chinos, while the girls wore dresses like lamp shades. Despite my near accident, my diving ability was not too bad, because I took lessons in Miami, where the instructor dumped all the equipment into the deep end of a pool and said to dive in, and put on while still under water. On the second attempt, I succeeded. The secret was to grab the weight belt and the mouthpiece of the scuba tank, then clear the mask and so on. Due to all the excitement, the journey home was two week later that planned and to add to the mystique, the return was by another Queen Ship, the Queen Mary.

CHAPTER 3

California and Hawaii

Now three years had passed since I was last in the States. I had saved hard for a return trip, but this time with surfing in mind! In September 1965, I purchased the flight and a Greyhound bus ticket – $99 for 99 days. This was good for tourists only, and as it was considered great value, the deal soon became advertised as $99 for just two weeks. My trip was partially to attract business for the hotel. This meant that I had to call into travel agents in New York, Boston, Cleveland and San Francisco and display the hotel brochures for their consideration while pounding the streets in 80 degrees Fahrenheit, all the time trying to look fresh and well dressed in my best Boston suites. Eventually in San Francisco after all was done I finally got into shorts and headed by tram to the coast and the beach near Fleishaker Park and the Golden Gate Recreation Area. The day was hot and sultry, the beach was shelving and resembled our Killiney Strand. The waves were shoulder high with almost no wind. As I did not have a board, I approached a group of teens and asked to borrow theirs. Looking back, it was amazing, because their answer was in the affirmative, and it came with a smile.

The board was the standard ten feet with a large 'skeg' – as fins were called in those days. It was covered in soft wax with an odour of sweet perfume, the like of which I had never experienced. So, with confidence I paddled out for my first ever fibreglass board experience. It was much lighter than the logs that I had built and it turned as I wanted. The sea was just like at home except warmer and so I did not need a wetsuit. Once out beyond the break, I turned the board for shore and paddled in front of an unbroken swell. The board felt trim and steady and I stood up immediately while leaning to the right. The swell held up, allowing time for me to traverse its face. I held this trim position for all of five seconds and then swung directly towards shore as the wave heaved over behind me. I knew I had taken a good ride and that those lads would have noticed everything without even looking up. Then, to my surprise, I acted really cool and did not attempt another ride, but returned the board and thanked the boys. It looked like I knew what I was doing, or perhaps that the waves were not up to my standard. If only they really knew I was just quitting while ahead. I'm sure I would have botched the next ride if attempted.

Oahu

Compelled by the lure of the islands, and the history of Pearl Harbour, I visited a travel agent, where the lady quoted me one hundred dollars each way to Honolulu. In a flash, I thought of the island's surfing tradition, Tom Blake and Duke Kahanamoku, and felt I might never tread this way again. Therefore, on 2nd October 1965, I went the extra mile and booked a flight to Oahu. Before going, I bought a water skier's buoyancy aid to keep alive in big waves. I learned later that it was not a good idea and it was almost never used.

The island of Oahu looked like a gem as we descended from the blue heavens. Honolulu International Airport was awash with troops dressed in khakis, many carrying olive-green duffle bags on their way to and from Vietnam. The air was a solid 80 degrees and I knew for sure I had made the right decision.

I booked into the YMCA and met a guy from New York called Vic. He suggested we should share the hire of a car and I agreed.

28

Vic was all 'pow' as he worked for Pan Am and had won a flight to anywhere. He had therefore booked a free round-the-world tour and had five more days to complete it. We hired a Mustang convertible, which was the 'in car' for young people at the time, and buzzed all over the place. Vic tutored me in American driving while yelling 'Keep in your lane!' and so on. Our trip included a visit to Hotel Street, which was another sea of khaki or white uniforms. Most, if not all, of these guys were also on their way to Nam, as the war was escalating at the time. The bars featured go-go dancers, some in cages and others on the counters. It was a fun scene but we just downed one drink, looked, laughed and left.

Vic departed the following day and said that I should hang on to the car. Later, as I drove towards Pearl Harbour to have a look, a Marine thumbed a ride and I stopped. He was Sergeant Jiminez and he was full of blarney and took me through gate check and directly onto an atomic submarine, which was in dock. Then he showed the hospital that had been strafed by the Japanese on that day of infamy in 1941. It had been left as a monument and was still full of bullet holes. In those days Waikiki Beach was fringed with lots of palms and a large colony of one-storey beach huts, in which families from the mainland dwelt while enjoying a native-style life. Today the area is filled with twenty-storey buildings.

Diamond Head, which is an extinct volcano, protrudes into the turquoise sea. It was with that island backdrop that I went surfing. I bought a pair of flowery board shorts, hired a tourist-type board at the beach, rubbed it with the perfumed wax and surfed in two-foot waves. I also tried 'Queens' in the morning and then hired another board down at 'Canoes' and surfed the spot called 'Poplars'. This was the zenith of life, as all sorts of people of all ages, decked in floral jams, were bowling towards shore with the greatest of ease. Leaves floated in the water and there was a scent in the air – maybe it was wax and sun lotion! The surf was the most pleasant I had ridden so far – no cold, no wetsuits, no fear. I caught turquoise waves with creamy curls that rolled for hundreds of yards. The paddle out was in crystal-clear water and it felt like paradise. The boards were twelve feet long and as the waves broke slowly, they were easy to catch. Some of surfers there that day, probably lived in the beach colony and for them it must have felt like there was no tomorrow. By now my surfing had taken a big leap forward, because I was now able to walk to the nose of the board with ease. I visited the open-air market by the beach and bought a large poster of George Downing surfing at Sunset Beach, Hawaiian LPs, several 8mm surfing movies, more board shorts, a luau shirt and lastly a grass skirt with a ticket to assure the purchaser that it was inflammable! All this was to come in useful at a later date.

Sunset Beach

Next day I re-hired a board and jammed it nose downwards into the back seat of the open-top Mustang. Being so long, it was quite a spectacle, but in those days, it didn't seem to bother anyone. In fact, it was quite fashionable, and I was only one of many. The goal was Sunset Beach, attractive because I knew George Downing surfed there and it looked exciting. Enroot, I stopped at Makapuu, famous for body boarding. From there I could see the reef breaking at Makai a little further north. I made my way there, driving down a rough path to the beach. The waves were about two to three feet and breaking about two hundred yards from shore, and it was busy with natives riding on anything they could find. One fellow was using half a board yet doing very well. It would be a long paddle out, but I went for it just the same. There was an onshore wind that made the waves sloppy like I was used to at home. I caught a few bumpy rides and got bounced all over the place. This was not as sweet as Waikiki, and as I had quite a distance to go, I came in and continued my lone surfari.

Next, I must have driven past the 'Banzai Pipeline' without knowing, because Sunset Beach was my target. The pipeline is famous for steep, hollow near-to-shore waves that break over coral and immensely difficult to ride. It's just as well I passed it by! It was about 2 p.m. when my white Mustang arrived at Sunset Beach.

The waves looked small but were breaking on the other side of the bay, over at a rocky promontory on the right. Then I noticed dots on these waves, and realised that they were surfers, so maybe the waves were rideable after all! I therefore carried my twelve-foot fibreglass plank down the steep beach, noticing that there were very few people around. As the water was flat I had a leisurely paddle across the bay. With each stroke, the highly buoyant board glided like a boat. On closer inspection, the waves began to look larger than I had previously thought. Now they looked about eight feet, but further in towards the rocky promontory they seemed to be twice that size and spilling over with great force. I watched with fascination as a brawny lad in board shorts flew down the face of an overhead curl and effortlessly swung his board to his right and sped across its face. He ended in the deeper water close to where I was positioned. All the others, about ten in all, were young, concentrating on the waves and hardly looked in my direction.

I finally arrived at Makapu, Oahu in 1965. The
Makai reef can be seen far beyond.

There was a lull in the waves, and so I moved nearer to where the surfers were clustered. Just then a big set came marching towards us. Luckily, it looked like I was to one side of the critical breaking area, and in line with the less threatening part of the wave. I might get to ride it, turn to my right, and beat it back into the deep. If I went the other way, I would end up on the rocks. The approaching wave loomed above me as if it was about to peel over. I looked to see whether there was anyone already riding it's exploding peak and coming at me from the left, but there wasn't, so I immediately paddled towards shore as fast as possible. Perhaps it was because I had an extra-long board that the wave picked me up. With flailing arms, I jumped to my feet and slid down its face. There was an enormous crashing sound and I went ripping across a blue, hollowing wall and heading for open water as if my life depended on it. Behind, a roaring curl chased me as if it had a powdery paw that would swipe me from behind. However, I was just ahead and getting filled with relief. The big board did all the work as I just crouched and hoped for the best. Then, in a merciful release, I zoomed out into the deep having had a ride of about a hundred yards – and all within seconds. I let out a muffled shout of joy and thought, if only my folks could have seen that! Of course, I didn't want the tough guys to know that I thought my ride was good. They would probably just have laughed.

Now the game was on and I had to try that again. I got back to the same position during a lull and managed to get another similar ride. With my ego expanding, I went out for more, but this time paddled closer to the point. I was now really in with the boys and therefore made the mistake of asking how high the waves were today. The guy looked at me critically and said,

'Twelve feet, have you ever been here before?'

Then without waiting for a reply he paddled away. The next set approached and most of the boys disappeared down its face. Then it was my turn, one, two, three, and I went paddling down a very steep face. The nose of the board dug deep in the concave trough and I went catapulting head-first downwards. With a ghastly thud I hit the water, plunging down so deep that all went dark. I was spun in all directions and did not know which direction was up. I was afraid of hitting the coral seabed and thought maybe I was done for! As there were no leashes in those days the board was automatically lost. This is where one's swimming experience can pay off. After what seemed like an eternity I managed to surface, only to see a second wave bearing down from above. I was thrashed another time and again sent helplessly spinning in the depths below. By divine intervention or the grace of King Neptune, I managed to break the surface, panting feverishly for blessed air and thinking, now where is my board before I'm hit again? Then I saw it floating about a hundred yards inside in the deep water. I struck out with all my might and swam as if in a race. None of the brawny boys took any notice; perhaps they were glad to see me punished and eliminated. As luck had it, I retrieved my board, but decided quit while ahead: two to one in my favour! While all this was going on there was a steady stream of Globe masters taking off from Kahuku Point military airfield, and turning towards the orient. The occupants were probably some of the same guys we had seen living it up in Hotel Street a few nights before. Some of them may have been looking down with envy and some might never return.

Sadly, I turned in my beloved Mustang at Honolulu International Airport, and amidst tourists, troopers and locals in luau shirts, I boarded a flight for L.A. and home.

Bray Ireland Surf Club

On my return from North America in 1965, I went into a sort of a downer. I missed the coffee, the cars and fast highways, contrasting with the open country and the friendly, unassuming folk. I still loved the simplicity of Ireland and the tranquillity that seeped throughout the land, but being young I could not deny the attraction of the big picture. I continued to send Surfer magazine loads of photos addressed to the editor, Pat McNulty. He was always polite and acknowledged my persistent bundles, out of which he did select a few for publication. Pat never mention that he was second-generation Irish at the time but later is seems that was why he kept up communication. But time was running out, and if I did not establish a proper club soon surfing might amount to nothing and fade out of sight. So, in a mild state of desperation I advertised the club in the Irish Independent newspaper's special notices section.

'What's this?' my Dad said, holding the paper.

'It says here that someone with our phone number is advertising something called Bray Ireland Surf Club.'

'Yes, that's my project!' I admitted proudly.

'Well,' he said, 'I hope you know what you are doing. It sounds crazy to me. Does your mother know about it?'

Nevertheless, putting that episode aside, there was some response to the advert. By now the club had a letterhead and envelopes. It had an image of Paul Strauch surfing an invisible wave. I also used the words 'Bray' and 'Ireland' so it would be known abroad. The first disciples to get in touch were Willie Hurst from Dublin, another Willie – Willie Parks from Strandhill, and Jean Parks, Willie's cousin, and Helena Condon, also from that area but studying in Dublin. My old pal Jurek was sort of half-interested, and so was Colm and a girl called Mary. In Greystones, there was Susan Fawcett and she sounded gung ho. Then, like a bolt out of the blue, two very important people got in touch. The phone rang and it was a guy with an American accent.

'Hi, I'm Tom Casey and I've surfed in Long Island and I'm a student in UCD. I'm interested in your club.'

This was great news; an American who surfed was just what we needed to give the club a western flavour. The newspaper advertisement was working. Then I got a call from Patrick Kinsella, who was now in sixth year at Blackrock College and concerned about his Leaving Cert exams. Despite this, Pat's friend had built a short eight-foot hollow board, and Pat could use it when he wanted. His friend had now more or less given up the idea of surfing and that suited the purpose. Pat was one step ahead and being enthusiastic he already had plans to get a job in Cornwall so as to learn how to make boards.

In addition, there was Dorothy Gilmore, a swimming instructor who had an encouraging laugh that put everyone in good humour. Also, Noel Haughey who owned a Citroen car that fascinated the 'clubbies' as it rose on its springs when the engine was turned on – just like Johnny Lee's family wagon. There was also Rodney Touch and Eric Fox, both Dubliners who knew Brittas Bay and the east coast quite well. So we all got together in Mount Herbert and we formalised Bray Ireland Surf Club. Needless to say, Surfer magazine was immediately informed. Then a letter arrived from Alan Duke from Portrush saying he and Davie Govan of Portstewart wanted to join the club. They also introduced Charlie Adjey, Davie Pierce and most Martin Lloyd who expanded his memory of those past times:

'It's hard to convey the complete obsession that I had with surfing or even the extreme physical highs or even, dare I say, spiritual experiences, which I still have to this day. I find it hard to imagine how life would have been without surfing. It has given so much pleasure and so much good company over forty-five years, not to mention it keeps one fit.'

'I got my first board from a fellow called Bo Vance who was based in Belfast. This is a one of the first polyester on styrene 'mistakes', as much of the foam disappeared leaving one to ride a sinking shell. However, I took it out in the sea at Rosbeg, Co.

Donegal – wearing, I might add, a yellow bathing cap, black long-sleeved T-shirt and Speedos just to be sure I kept warm!'

Now let us not lose sight of Ian Hill who, in that same year of 1965, was transferred back across the Irish Sea to Plymouth, where he remained for some years. Ian was sad to go and bade his gallant bunch of pioneer's goodbye, vowing he would return. In the meantime, he got married and they had a son called Andy, who would become a surf shop owner and legend in the Irish surfing scene. Ian got to surf a lot in Cornwall and then in 1979, true to his word, he returned for good to take up Irish surfing where he left off.

At the same time, Eddie Stewart from Dunmore East was by now quite advanced in surfing and had already visited and surfed some of the future hot spots. He told me he was not joining the club because in 1965 he went to Australia, where he surfed long boards in Queensland and out west. The surfing network was spreading!

First Fibreglass Board

1966 might have seemed like an age of innocence, but for the fact that Ireland had a bank strike that lasted almost six months and another to follow. Words cannot describe the deadly effect this had on businesses. One measure to overcome the difficulty was, how a factory in Bray, exchanged their cheques for our cash so as to pay their wages. We lodged their cheques when the strike was over. Unfortunately, by then many had gone out of business when the banks opened and personal indebtedness had risen.

However, not everything in '66 was contaminated, as we the club members were filled with continued surfing enthusiasm. But, alas, our boards were still out of date and it was paramount that something was done. The answer came in the form of the parish priest! One-day Father Tom McDowell, the Bray PP, was socialising with my Dad. They were sitting in the hotel lounge having coffees.

My Dad also had a glass of brandy and was in a really good mood and told McDowell about the club and his son's efforts to surf. McDowell was enjoying a Cuban cigar and in a haze of blue smoke, called me over to join them saying,

'I hear from your Dad that you are starting up surf club. Do you have the right equipment?'

Now feeling quite at ease, I told him about building wooden boards and that I had over spent and now could not afford fibreglass. To my amazement, the Padre replied,

'How much will a fibre board cost?'

'They cost about twenty-five pounds.'

'Look,' he responded, 'you are young and have maybe forty years left in you and spread over that time it's less than ten shillings a year and that's good value – money well spent!'

To make matters really comical, now my Dad was agreeing. So, as it turned out, good old Father Mac had pointed me in the right direction. As a direct result, I did as the Vatican bid me, and placed an order for a ten-foot custom board with that same Dough Wilson guy of Bilbo Surfboards in Cornwall. It cost twenty-eight pounds sterling delivered, but worth it, I hoped! However, before it arrived, one more rather urgent step had to be taken.

CHAPTER 4

Boat Show 1966

By now, there had been enough non-productive activity, and it was time to tell Ireland aloud, that surfing had arrived in the country. The best place to do that would be at the 1966, Royal Dublin Society, Irish Boat Show, that is, if we could just get a place. This great emporium comprised of a series of halls suitable for conventions and for horticultural events and would attract a multitude. After several phone calls the new club was accepted, and for a very small fee we were offered a balcony space with an electrical power point to show our wares.

The question was what would we display? My fibreglass board had not yet arrived. The originals, Mark I and II, had been damaged, but there was the balsa board and just maybe the hollow wooden model that Pat Kinsella's friend had hammered together. In desperation I had an idea, phoned the Irish Red Cross, and was delighted to discover that they had a large paddleboard. With their permission, I collected it and had it mounted in the centre of the display.

I had written to Pat McNulty to tell about the launching at the RDS. Perhaps it was the ghost of George Freeth doing a good turn because, to my surprise, Pat responded with a load of posters with the compliments the magazine's owner, John Severson. Now we had one two-by-four poster of Greg Noll at Waimea, standing in long striped trunks like pyjamas holding a huge board. There was also a Californian surfer at sundown and a shot from the pipeline, among others. We had that infamous A3 picture of George Downing riding a fifteen-foot wall at Sunset Beach, the very same picture that had spurred me to go there in '65. Then, to bring it all down to earth, there were photos that I had taken of surfing in Ireland, along with a map of the island with surf spots highlighted. Then there was some fun as Susan Fawcett and Colm helped deck the life-size cut-out Agfa girl in garlands and the Hawaiian-bought grass skirt. Veebee (very beautiful), as they called her, gave the stand that little bit of Aloha it so badly needed. As a finishing touch, I borrowed my Dad's 8mm projector and movie screen. Then I could show the surfing movies I had bought in Waikiki. As they were very spectacular and something brand new, people were impressed. So, for five days we showed surf movies, played Hawaiian melodies and Beach Boys music. The L.P.'s supplied by Pat Kinsella, as he was very up to date. The combined effect of music, Tom Casey's Long Island accent, our boards and my periodic puffing of cherry blend tobacco in a corn cob pipe all added to the ambiance we sought.

There was a lot of interest from other exhibitors, including Derek Martin who was selling kayaks and Rana boats from Norway. He kindly donated a 'Buckflex' wetsuit to the club. But some of the other stands were manned by older laid-back fellows in blazers who looked at the surf stand in horror. There was quite a flood of school kids, many lured by the music. There was also a lot of buzz about the first ever surfing safari that was planned for Easter. Then on the last day, a meeting as important as Stanley's with Dr Livingstone occurred. It came in the form of a tall, youthful-looking English fellow of about thirty. He was wearing a tweed sports coat and appeared delighted to have stumbled on the location. He smiled and said, 'Excuse me, but I am interested in your club. You see, I have just arrived to live in Ireland and have a fibreglass board in the docks.'

This was Roger Steadman, who would contribute so much to the sport in Ireland. The effect of Roger's contact was dynamic. Tom and I looked at each other.

Tom hissed, 'Kev, did you hear what he said? – he has a fibreglass board!'

With that, a lifelong friendship between Roger and I came into being. Here was the sort of person who could shape the future of the club, and what's more he already had a board! Unfortunately, as the official club 'Surfari' was just a week away so Roger could not come. He explained that had just bought a house and was taking possession. He and his wife Rosemary had two young girls, Claire and Elizabeth. Rosemary was originally from Guernsey and so understood island living; settling in Ireland would not present a problem. Roger had been transferred by Unilever and had all the qualities of a great manager and the dash that would make him one of Ireland's finest surfers. Meeting Roger was also a portal to tapping other great people for the club in the months that followed. This was a great step forward, as now people with a firm business background had come on board. Finally, the Boat Show got good press and the stand took in lots of applications, out of which, only a half dozen joined. That's how things always are – nothing comes easy!

Colm remembers how he enjoyed working on the Boat Show stand:

'Yes, there was a clipboard where people who were interested in joining the surf club could fill out their details. I filled out the details for every female that passed our stand. They gave their name, address and the phone number. It was like lambs to the slaughter. One full stop after their name was Morse code for nice, two dots meant very nice and three dots was magnificent. Yes, I remember it well. It took the whole of the following winter to work my way through the list. Mind you a fair proportion of them told me to hump off when I rang!'

The Club exhibit stand at the RDS March 1966. Tom Casey is holding a Surfer Magazine on display beside our Agfa Aloha girl.

CHAPTER 5

The first ever Surfari

Just after the Boat Show, word came that my board had arrived at Dublin Docks. I horridly collected it and breathlessly laid the package out on the gravel in front of the family home. Then I began the process of tearing off the cardboard. To my delight, out slid a magnificent red board from Bilbo with two parallel white stripes from nose to tail. When I went to lift it I discovered how very heavy it was, but regardless of that I was delighted to have a proper board at last. Immediately after that I wrote to Bilbo and said I would like to become their Irish agent. I hoped for a favourable reply, but I had to wait.

My Dad, while wearing a flower in his lapel, had kindly agreed to cover my duties for the Easter weekend. I guess that makes him one of our early benefactors. The only people prepared to drop everything and come on the Easter trip were my brother Colm, Tom Casey from Montauk, and Patrick Kinsella, who was worried about doing his Leaving Cert exams in a couple of months' time. Colm asked why it was not called a safari? Tom explained it would be a surfing safari, a cross between Swahili and Beach Boy jargon. This appealed to Pat, who was captivated and wanted to get 'in the groove'.

I was now the proud owner of a second-hand, dark green 1964 Vauxhall Victor 101 station wagon. It was as tough as a Panzer and ideal for the trip. The roof rack was made of iron and permanently welded to the roof. We got ready for battle and all that was needed were the boards. So, we loaded my new fibreglass board, the now red balsa board and Kinsella's hollow wooden board, and tied them on with coils of heavy rope. We climbed in and left for Sligo via the city. It Holy Week of 1966, we drove through Dublin at early morning rush hour feeling very proud to be sporting such a fine bunch of boards tied to the roof.

As we drove I thought about the weight of my new board. Now I had a professionally designed board, but I wondered why it was so heavy. Perhaps they had used a dense Styrofoam as core, or maybe Bilbo reckoned I would need a log for Irish waves, or maybe they reckoned that I wouldn't know any better and would just sell it on! Then, amidst grunts, one liners and mutterings the little band of sea-coast warriors headed north-west, aiming for the most likely place to have a wave. That target area was Strandhill, Co. Sligo because our Ordnance Survey map showed it was facing the whole of the north Atlantic. We soon found that Donegal Bay was fringed with a seventy miles of wave prone beaches, reefs and points – it could become a surfing Mecca, and it did.

If we stopped enroot, people stared with curiosity, and one person asked if those things were tractor blades? In no time, we were out on the open road and blazing into the north-west using what would later be the M4, but then, just a narrow, twisted road with few straight sections. As we went, Tom entertained the car with cowboy and Beach Boy songs and finally his favourite party piece, 'The Mayor of Bayswater'. Tom's rich baritone voice rose and fell like the bumps on the road, as it was already smoothed with rum that he brought in a hip flask. The trip was off to a good start!

Surfari Reaches Co. Sligo

We arrived on the Sligo coast under the shadow of the steep slopes of Knocknarea. This is one of several flat-topped mountains that reminds many of South Africa's Table Mountain. Below this, facing north-west and stretching down to the sea, lies was the village of Strandhill, or an Leathros in Irish.

Spread left and right of the town, was a golden beach that seemed like a barrier holding back the mighty ocean. Over to its right, the bay sweeps out in a curve to finish at a point called Blue Rock and Coney Island. Looking in the other direction, there are massive dunes and a coastline running perpendicular to meet an estuary, beyond which are the rolling hills of County Mayo. We speedily descended the hill and went through the town. The day was windless and benign, with cloud cover like mother of pearl. Then we finally got to see the beach and found the sea was at about half tide, and sultry waves of about three feet were breaking, just to welcome us. Out on Coney Island we could see perfect lines peeling off at perhaps the same three feet. About a thousand yards out to the left there were nice waves breaking, and we later learned that underneath there was a hard-packed turf bottom; it was really a Gaelic-style reef. There was a wide parking area and a massive cannon gun from the Armada days pointing to the horizon – but so far, no one in sight! This was like the movie High Noon and we were the rustlers coming to shoot up the waves and everyone was indoors, perhaps peeping out at our arrival. In fact nothing was further from the truth; our presence went completely unnoticed except by Willie Parks, who knew we were coming but could not manage to be there.

Tom let out a whoop.

'Look, we got waves, not very large but nice. We are about to do some real surfing!'

Without a further word we untied the boards, and donned our patchy wetsuits, not considering for a moment that poor young Pat had nothing but a grey tracksuit top. Tom and I went out first and had turns on the new Bilbo. The sea was winter-cold but we were too excited to notice. We noted that the Bilbo had been shaped by someone called Rod Sumpter. Written on the stringer was his code, number 89, and I remembered reading about him in Surfer magazine. There was no challenge from the sea that day, just polite waves suitable for these beginners – as that is what we really were.

On that momentous day, I remember paddling on my knees until I was positioned in front of an approaching wave; then I caught my first fibreglass board ride in Ireland. It was just like the San Francisco experience, but this time I manoeuvred, allowing for a trip across its green wall. Another wave presented itself and with barely enough time, I turned and paddled hard and repeated the performance before handing the board back to Tom. Now Tom displayed his Long Island experience by driving the board into places on the waves that I had never thought possible. Tom could even walk the deck and dangle one foot over the nose without falling off. He put life back into those sleepy waves and caused the lads on shore to whistle and shout.

Peering out at the waves watching Tom gave me the chance to think about how the rails of the board act on waves and how the fin gives direction. In Hawaii, I barely had time to think like that. All efforts were to save my life on each ride and frantic paddling to retrieve my lost board. Here surfing was more relaxed, and enjoyable in a more technical kind of way. When the deed was done and everyone was satisfied, we looked for a place to stay. We went to the only obvious establishment, the Baymount Hotel (since demolished) and talked to Mr Byrne, the owner. He was a true hotelier and welcomed us in. He immediately embraced the concept of surfing, and made us feel like heroes instead of vagabonds, adding tales about the local waves. He said that the turf-laden sandbanks often made the swell break far out and suggested, 'Some day you should go out in a boat with a board, to ride it.'

Then he offered us an excellent rate for the accommodation and opened his bar. As we did not have much spare cash we were not much use to him in that respect. Next day, we headed north after studying the coast on an Ordnance Survey map. We drove north to Grange and stopped for Gas. Another man called Willie was the owner of the then-named 'Willie's Gas Station'. We asked him about Streedagh Strand and how we could get there. Would you believe, he actually closed his station, came with us and showed how, at low tide, to cross the estuary and get to the dunes from the rear. Willie even helped carry the board and waited while we surfed the choppy waves. So, we thanked him, and he went to his garage and we went to survey the cliffs nearby. Oddly, we noticed lots of a silicone-like substance flowing out of the slate-like rocks in the area. We jested that maybe there was oil below. It turned out to be algae, but to this day I often wonder! On passing, we dropped in and said goodbye to Willie, and thanked him. Later he became a prominent councillor in the region and his business thrived, till he sold it and retired. In recent years I called in to see him in the retirement home in 2007, but as his memory was affected he had difficulty recalling events, liked being appreciated.

First Surfboards to Rossnowlagh

Next day it was bright, chilly yet sunny, and we continued north to Rossnowlagh. This area consists of a broad beach that sweeps north in a gentle curve for about a mile. There is a headland at the south end, topped with a few guesthouses and in later years an excellent restaurant called Smugglers Creek. Several miles distant and to the north, there is a rib of rocks running out to sea for at least a quarter of a mile, beyond it lies St John's Point, all which partly blocks swell from the north-west. The beach therefore picks up swells mainly from the west or south-west, and because of its long, sandy shore it generates good waves.

Our band of brothers arrived by way of the coast road around the southern headland blessed with a Franciscan friary. This is a place of refuge where people come from miles around to make a retreat. From our lofty perch, we gazed at the scene below. It was a pristine view of tiny walls of water forming in lines and marching in from quite a distance. Tom let out another whoop, perhaps because it looked so inviting, but certainly not because the surf was big!

'Let's hit it, guys!' he shouted, and in hypnotic obedience we rallied to the cause. We descended a steep road from the cliffs, and drove like bandits along the beach. The tide was out and we stopped in line with the Sandhouse Hotel, the only building on the skyline. We prepared for the historic occasion by taking another photograph. This time it was Tom and me standing with the two boards upright. Pat was sitting on the beach with a strange ball of something in his hand. It was candle wax for rubbing on the deck of the boards so we would not slip off. Colm was the photographer, and did a good job.

The First Surfari arrives at Rossnowlagh. Left to right, Myself with balsa board and Tom Casey with new fibreglass board. Pat Kinsella is sitting, while holding a ball of candle wax for the boards. Propper surf wax was not available. Photo by Colm Cavey.

Now it was time to get into that icy ocean. Once again, we frolicked in the waves, and this time I broke out my Dad's 8mm movie camera and began recording. The wetsuits were not very insulated but we carried on in a state of suspended consternation, each one using his enthusiasm as a barrier to the cold. Pat amazed us again by taking rides wearing only an anorak for protection. None of us had the decency to loan our wetsuits to him. Tom commandeered the fibreglass board and began to mimic big-wave riders with some quick take-offs, his suit tail flapping behind him as the fashion in California used to be. All this was filmed (See dvd Dawn.) After an hour, we gave up the ghost and hurriedly dressed into our chilly clothes.

'Now, guys, my folks know the Britton family so let's call in to their hotel.'

I suggested this while pointing at the majestic building on the skyline. We drove up there and gingerly entered the lobby, which was ever so quaint with plush carpeting and oil paintings with gilded frames and a welcoming fire burning in an old-fashioned fireplace. A tall, elegant lady with blonde hair and a welcoming smile approached. It was nice of her to smile even though we looked completely out of place in her magnificent surroundings. I spoke quickly, and introduced myself and friends for fear that she would eject us before a word could be passed.

'Boys, meet Mrs Mary Britton, the owner of this fine hotel.'

She responded by asking about my family. She added that she had seen the car on the beach and wondered what we had been doing. She might have said 'I know what you were doing', I cannot quite remember. After a quick explanation she called her husband, Vinnie. Almost immediately a man appeared. He was of medium height and had a weather-beaten face with a steely stare that we discovered, soon enough, masked his lighted-hearted humour. He was dressed in dusty clothes and told us he had just added an extension to the hotel, which he had built himself. Then, with a calculating eye, he settled down to hear our tale.

I felt like we were about to try and sell cattle to a farmer at the local market. I lost all sense of 'hep', and my surfer-style accent was reduced to a sort of babble punctuated by nervous giggles. I reckoned Vinnie would never understand what I was saying. However, when my spiel concluded, he sat back and drew a breath. There was silence for a moment. A vacuum cleaner could be heard buzzing in the distance, while the flickering of the fire in the hallway added to the drama.

'Well, lads,' he said, 'I think you are onto something!'

His words were music to our ears and a boost to the morale.

'I have five boys and lots of hotel guests and I'd be interested in hearing more from you about your boards. I might buy a few. What will they cost?' I assured him that I could supply the boards and they would cost £25 each delivered. He immediately agreed. I could not manage hiding a big grin and a pair of happy feet, as I led the three merry men out to the car.

If we could have seen into the future we would have learned that the Sandhouse Hotel would eventually become the hub of surfing in Ireland and be referred to in jest as the 'Britton Empire'. That Brian, his eldest, would become president of the future Irish Surfing Association and of the European Surfing Federation. Barry, his brother, would open an interior/exterior design shop adjacent to the hotel, David would become an art dealer in Dublin, Conor would open a restaurant on the adjacent cliffs and William would open a fish farm in Donegal Bay. Not possessing the faculty of foresight, however, yet confident that something magnificent was brewing; we bade the Britton's goodbye and headed up the Donegal coast. The reaction of the Britton's spurred me to a more vigorous pursuit of serious board importation. (Our surfing that day is recorded in the movie 'Dawn' which is available on youtube.)

Barry was the third-eldest lad of the Britton family. He became an architect and design artist and works from offices in Rossnowlagh.

He and his wife Emcee had a daughter named Easkey who would later become a legend in the surfing world. Not only did she become Irish Women's Champion, but would also take a quantum leap further than most would dare. Looking back, Barry said:

'My mother, universally known as 'Mrs B', acquired two Malibu surfboards for her hotel on the beach at Rossnowlagh, for use of her hotel guests. Once the Britton boys set eyes on them, that was it – we were hooked! To the end of her days, Mrs B regretted bringing those surfboards into her Grade A four-star hotel and turning her nice well-behaved boys into a bunch of no-star beach bums. Mrs B had witnessed the early sixties in California first-hand while on promotional tours for the Irish tourist board – Bord Fáilte. I know Kevin Cavey also made promotional tours to the States; it was the practice of the hoteliers of that era. Then when, by coincidence, Kevin and co. came knocking on the Sandhouse Hotel door, on that cold crisp Easter week-day, having already surfed the beach, she already knew what they were up to and promptly placed an order for boards.

Surfari Heads Northwards

Perhaps we resembled a moment selected out of the future. Just imagine a brigade of 'Recon Marines', the spearhead of an invasion, bouncing their way forward in Humvees with Baghdad as their target. We were travelling vaguely under similar conditions; driving in a poorly sprung vehicle, damp, cramped and uncomfortable, but determined to go somewhere at all costs! Our only attribute was the camaraderie and the humour; otherwise there was little to offer. As we headed north our first stop was Ardara and a visit to the local church for Easter ceremonies. The lads were not too impressed with my diversion but I was the driver and we could pray for surf. After investigating the Donegal coast, we were attracted by the city lights, and therefore headed for some vibrant student action in Portrush on the Antrim coast. This town was a hive of activity where we encountered hundreds of the north of Ireland's university

50

students enjoying the Easter Break. 'This towns on fire,' exclaimed Colm. The girls were plentiful and quite magnificent, and we were agog, but first things first. We located a B & B on Causeway Street and convinced the landlady that we were starving, which was not difficult as we were like desperados. She in her goodness produced four enormous Northern Ireland fries. After that was consumed, for some reason best known to Tom Casey, he took a blanket from his bed, wrapped it around himself and paraded out on the town. He looked like Indian from a Sioux camp or maybe a sailor from a shipwreck. We followed suit, and soon the 'four amigos' went out to case the town, all without the landlady even noticing. Either way this tactic gave us an image, brought on conversation with the girls and caused us to laugh for the whole evening. Naturally, we returned the blankets intact.

Next day I looked up my surfing contact notes and went to Alan Duke's house, also on Causeway Street. Alan has already been mentioned as one of the dawn surfers in Northern Ireland. Unfortunately, Alan was not there and did not know we were coming. Another early contact was Desmond 'Bo' Vance, but he lived in Belfast. We had already alerted the local Antrim newspaper, so we phoned them on arrival and they sent a photographer join us on the East Strand. He took some details and a photo of us surfing. The shot was distant, but it did announce that surfing was already on the cards!

That night we went to the dance in a big ballroom by the seafront. Yep, in those days there were no clubs or discos, and big bands were the thing. We rock 'n' rolled the evening away with nurses from Altnagelvin hospital, and students from Queens. However, despite the fun, next day, all was not well, as Pat was thinking about his studies and was weighing up the sacrifice he had made against his future. And it did not add up! He became disillusioned and began, saying, 'I want to go home, this is a dreadful surfari.' Then he would launch into the Beach Boys' number:

'I wanna go home. I wanna go home, I feel so broke up, I wanna go home.'

So, Pat was right, and we had better go. We decided to return to Dublin via Belfast, but it was now quite late and we were short of gas, mainly because we were running out of cash. At about 7 p.m., as we hurled along a narrow hedge-lined road, I fell fast asleep at the wheel. This was not noticed as the others were also in their slumbers. It was a sort of gradual demise that took over, as slowly my foot came off the accelerator. Then, at about 15 M.P.H., we ploughed into a ditch. The crew were jolted awake.

'You idiot, what were y' doin'?'

'I fell asleep, you don't think I did that on purpose?'

We clambered out and heaved and hauled, and then managed to reverse back on to the road. Somehow, we made it to Belfast and eventually home. Finally we limped through Dublin, unlike the warriors we had been on the outward journey, dropped Tom off in the city, and then left Pat to his home in Foxrock – where he removed his board from the roof, turned and said,

'Thanks guys, but I've got to get on with my life.'

He scurried away, never once looking back. When Colm was asked later about his surfing, he replied honestly:

'Never really did much surfing. I tagged along as the brother and did a lot of watching and taking photos from the shore. My friends were wide and varied and nearly all female.' [Chuckle] That brought the Great Surfari to its finality.

As an outcome of the trip, there was some unfinished business. I promptly wrote to Bilbo of Cornwall and said once again, that I would like their distributor as I had lots of customers who wanted boards and therefore would like to be their agent for Ireland. Bilbo agreed to supply boards at wholesale prices, but did not commit about the sole agency. The two boards requested by the Britton's were called 'pop outs' - ten feet long, quite wide, and coated in white fibreglass with stripes and decorations on the decks. Today Bic and other board makers produce 'pop outs' in all shapes and sizes, suitable for beginners and even experienced surfers.

CHAPTER 6

C&S Bilbo Surfboards Agency

Just three days later, while back at work and still dreaming of the week gone by, there was a phone call.

'Hello, this is Roger Steadman, we met at the Boat Show. Look, I am now settled in, and ready to come to your next meeting.'

I replied, 'Have you used your board yet?'

'No, did not have time.'

I was relieved and said, 'If you like we can have a meeting tomorrow at 8 p.m. in my house on Herbert Road.' This in effect meant throwing a meeting for Roger. But it would be worth it. I called up the members and that included Tom Casey who alarmed me with his response.

'I can't get to the meeting. You know I really enjoyed the surfari, but I have to go back to the States. I have been drafted. Look, it's been great hanging out with you guys, say adios to your brother and Pat Kinsella.'

I was speechless, and wondered why I was so upset at losing someone whom I hardly knew. In those few surfari days we had all bonded, but also his reason for departure was a tragedy. Roger arrived at Mount Herbert where he met Rodney Touch, Eric Fox and Johnny Lee, who was an Aer Lingus pilot. Roger told us that he also had a business friend, Harry Evans, who would be interested in the club. As it turned out, both Roger and Harry proved to be the two most essential elements in the development of the club, and indeed the sport in Ireland. Harry was ex British Army and had a very large family while his eldest daughter Vivienne, was destined to become Ireland's first girl surfer, but more about that later. Roger who was tall and lean and obviously a sportsman examined my newly arrived fibreglass board. Then from the top of his car he produced a magnificent cream-coloured equivalent. This one was about the same length as mine but infinitely lighter. Interestingly it had a few more curves in the right places, and that would enhance its performance. The meeting immediately decided on several follow-up surfaris that included Rossnowlagh, Sligo, Lahinch and Tramore – all to happen as soon as possible.

Next day Roger and I agreed that since we had both bought Bilbo boards, we should press again for a sole agency and that we should call our outfit C&S Surfboards, derived from 'Cavey and Steadman'. With Rogers's exposure to business and my blind enthusiasm, we made a convincing pair. Roger drafted a good sales pitch to Dough Wilson of Bilbo, to which we got an early reply agreeing to give us sole agency for Ireland. We were not sure if that included Northern Ireland but decided to leave that question aside. Unknown to us at the time, Bo Vance had secured that privilege but found that there was little financial return in it. We on the other hand were just interested in spreading the sport and the fun that went with that crusade. In or around May '66 our order arrived for Vinnie Britton and his lads. Roger and family delivered the boards to Rossnowlagh and were overcome with the surf and the reception they received. The story goes that when Roger arrived with the boards there was pandemonium. The boys were quite excited but in the euphoria, no one asked how and where they should be used. Roger presumed they knew all about the sport, but it turned out they did not. It was later learned that the boys used the boards in the local river but not in the sea. So, Barry recalled,

'Roger and Kevin felt they had a sort of duty of care to their customers, so Roger made a return trip to show us how surfing should be done giving us a demo with lots of tips on what to do and not to do. In the meantime, we saw this big Hawaiian-looking guy standing up on his Kookbox home-made surfboard, riding all the way to shore. It was Clive Davies from Enniskillen, who became our constant surf buddy until 1968 when the troubles broke out in Northern Ireland, causing Clive never to come south of the border again. I heard that Clive died a few years ago, but rumour has it that he spent some time mingling with the native Hawaiian beach boys of Honolulu and rode Waikiki with them, in true soulful Hawaiian style. Looking back, in the beginning we mostly surfed in the summer but then older brother Brian somehow wangled a diver's wetsuit. Sometimes you'd get the jacket, but other times you'd end up with the trousers and have to top it off with a thick Aran sweater!'

From that time, onwards a great Irish surfing dynasty was born. Soon after that Vinnie built and developed a Surfer's Bar in his hotel and filled it with memorabilia of the sport. This included the original invoice to Brian for a further custom board he bought from C&S for the sum of ir£36.

Roger also took a shine to Lahinch and returned from one of the trips in ecstasy over the quality and consistency of the waves. He also linked up with Johnny Lee, the pilot and they both brought their caravans and camped at the Liscannor and surfed while their kids wallowed in the sand dunes. Harry Evans and his wife Carmel caught on to the idea and joined in as often as possible. Mean time our board sales continued and one customer important was Pat Kinsella, who had got over his exams, saved his money and then ordered a royal blue and navy custom board which he rode with newly acquired expertise.

This board ended its days cut down by a quarter and residing in the Surfers Bar or somewhere locally at Rossnowlagh.

We began to order in O'Neill wetsuits from California. These would supplement our board sales, were very attractive and the rubber was very soft – no chafing of the skin. I tried one immediately as they came in short versions, which were great for summer surfing. A fellow called Willie Siddall, who had a scuba diving shop in Dalkey, also discussed the design requirement for Irish surfing wetsuits. We named them 'Eurosuits' and one of the features was a tube and mouthpiece, so one could breathe warm exhaled air back into the suit while waiting for the next winter wave. We sold a few for him, but later he dropped the idea, as it was too costly to produce.

Meantime, up north, boards were being built from scratch. Bo Vance saw how the sport was developing:

'Now at that time, while our fairly technical approach to building boards was being pursued by a small but growing band of us in the North, new followers were being recruited in the South, many buying boards from C&S and bypassing the arduous task of building their own and getting on with task of finding good surfing beaches.'

Stamina was a necessary component for a surfer. I obtained mine in a strange sort of way. Each year since I was sixteen I had been to Saint Patrick's Island, Donegal. My parents had introduced me to its hardships. The island in Lough Derg is where one fasts, prays and resides for two nights, and only sleeps for one. As well as spiritual values, one of the benefits of the experience is a self-belief that one could endure lasting hardship and if this was to be applied to surfing it might help. On one occasion, I drove to the island and brought my board along, intending to visit the Brittons in Rossnowlagh on the way home. When I finally staggered to my car I noticed with satisfaction that the board had not been stolen by some local who might want to use it to go fishing, or just to mend a gap. So, starving but very happy, I drove over the hills and down to Rossnowlagh. On arrival, the weather was benign and the waves shoulder-high and glassy – just right for a penitential. As it turned out, all the boys were away at school so I went out alone. I was quite amazed to find that I had no difficulty paddling out or riding the waves. That night I slept like never before and the next day enjoyed my first proper meal in seventy-two hours, capped it with more surfing, and then headed home.

Greystones

It was June 1966 and I was studying weather maps, expecting a strong bluster from the south-east. I was now 'board happy' and jumped at the opportunity to take advantage of impending large surf at Greystones Harbour. (1) Jurek came along and decided he would take a few photos. Therefore, he clambered out along the north wall. From that vantage point he could get some close-up shots. Up to then one had to spend endless time fighting the sea, often paddling for twenty minutes just to get outside beyond a break. However, this time it would be different, as I could paddle sideways into the waves through the mouth of the harbour.

On our arrival, the sea appeared quite large. Storm sets were coming from the south-east as predicted, and wheeled around the outer wall of the harbour and were rolling by the entrance. Therefore, wearing a very old wetsuit, I launched my brand-new Bilbo in the flat water inside the harbour and paddled out sideways into the fray. When I was well clear of the north wall, after crossing several large spilling swells, I turned and looked inland. The twin peaks of the Sugar Loaf Mountains loomed, as if watching my every move. Bray Head protruded to my right, and the north wall was on my immediate left with Jurek now perched on top. A set of extra-large waves arrived and I mumbled a quick Hail Mary. I let two of them pass but went for the third. I paddled hard and took off, on an unbroken peak, and jumped to my feet while cutting left. I slid faster than expected while traversing its face.

'Whee! This is great – but I should be going the other way,' I thought.

I frantically heaved hard to the right, the board responded just as the wave collapsed, and with that I was propelled towards shore. Just then I believe Jurek took a photo. The way was now clear for a long ride, and I was determined not to fall off. I stopped just short of the shore break which was thunderous. Despite the strong suction, I managed to clamber out still upright as some people smiled and went their way. I repeated the performance several times that day, till I ran out of mojo.

'Hey, Jurek, did you get a shot?

'Yeah, Horse, I think I did.'

'You know Jurek,' I said, 'in physics, if you look at a quantum wave it collapses. In surfing I think it's the opposite. If you were not here to observe then that first wave I rode was never there! It only happened in my imagination. So therefore, always have a friend with you when you surf.'

Jurek laughed. 'and a camera,' he said. Since then Greystones has lost it's wave for ever as a monstrous Marina has been built there - a tragedy!

Rodney

Rodney Sumpter was an Australian of English parent, and one of Cornwall's top surfers. He also claimed to have relatives in Waterford – or at least Watford! Rod was a shaper with Bilbo and shaped my first board and he therefore contacted me to say he would be over to check out the Irish scene. This came like a bolt out of the blue and put a new spin on our lives. Here was someone from the outside world taking a real interest in Irish surfing. It was a compliment. Rod arrived in Dublin Airport – or Collinstown, as it was then known. He was everything a surfer was supposed to be: tall, thin, smiling, and wearing a bright yellow canvas jacket with surf badges on the sleeves. He extended a firm sun-tanned hand and from that moment Ireland had made a true friend. He collected his board from the baggage table and mumble as he did so,

'Hey, I just put this board together for the trip, hope the glass is dry.'

I was so keen to see the board that he agreed and opened the bag for my inspection. There before my eyes was a bright red ten-foot board, with a large white patch on the deck. I lifted it and exclaimed, 'Rod, that's a good surfboard and it's so light not like my log.'

'Well, you see, I didn't bother with a stringer. You know, that strip of wood down the centre of every board to give it shape and strength. Well, it's not really necessary so I omitted it for speed and convenience.'

I was astounded.

Rod stayed with us that night and next day I gathered a few of the club members and we took him to nearest possible surf spot – Brittas Bay. In those days, there were no beach restrictions and we could enter a caravan park called McDaniel's and travel along the cliffs to select the best break. Though the waves were about two foot nothing Rod still got in and gave us a demo. He was so agile that he even did a headstand and a 'skeg' first take-off. That meant paddling for the wave with the board backwards. When the wave pushed the fin caught and the board spun around, nose first. To do this he had to be up on his feet at lightning speed and able to dance some ballet steps. We then took him to Malachy's pub for a traditional pint, as he had really earned it.

At the first opportunity I said, 'Rodney, I like your board: it's much lighter than mine.'

'Yep,' Rodney said with a grin. 'It's yours for twenty quid. I don't want to take it back with me.'

'A deal,' I squawked, and another pint was bought.

Next day we arranged a surfari for Rod, which meant that I drove him to St Stephen's Green, where we met three cars from the club, one of which would take him to Sligo. Because of work I could not go along and made a hasty retreat to the hotel. Weekends are always a difficult time to get off duty when one is in the hospitality industry. Rod found the surf in Strandhill to be about head high, with a light cross-wind. It seems that Rod caught some nice waves and as we had contacted the Sligo Champion newspaper beforehand, they took a photo of him surfing and put in their next edition. All this was in fulfilment of our calling to spread the word, which we believed was our passionate responsibility. Willie Parks later told me that Rod paddled out with the greatest of ease. He turned and picked successive three to four-foot walls and began to streak across them to his right, climbing and dropping and as he went. He finished each ride by cutting back and landing prone on the board already paddling back out for more. During this whole episode, the throng of onlookers increased by the minute.

On his return from the trip, as we were going to the airport, Rod said, 'Kev, that was a wonderful experience and you know I can't wait to return to your excellent waves.' That was the last I saw of Rod for two months. In the meantime, as usual, I reported all that had happened to Pat McNulty in Surfer magazine, and he told me in a letter that the 3rd World Surfing Championships would take place in San Diego, California, and did I think an Irish team would enter? This I told him was out of the question as it would be a gigantic undertaking and we were only at the teething stages of the sport in Ireland. However, from that moment onwards, I developed a passion to get there, and pestered the saints about it; not know how it could happen. When I told the members about the forthcoming event, they just laughed and I felt foolish for mentioning it.

CHAPTER 7

Surfari to Tramore

In June 1966, I tried Rod's new lightweight board at Greystones Harbour during a summer swell. I did some whips and turns on shoulder-high waves close to shore. Jurek was once again taking photos. It was sunny and I did not bother with a wetsuit because that did not look island-like, and I felt that's what this sport was about. When I clambered out and hobbled over the sharp stones, I heard a voice.

'Alo, I did not know you could do that in Ireland.'

I realised I had been addressed by a pretty French girl whom I had seen once before on the harbour. She and an American friend called Katherine Powers had been watching the performance. Katherine had on an earlier occasion taken a few photos of my attempts to wake board. However, I now wanted to impress them both, so I responded with a macho grunt.

'Ah, ye' know, we do it all the time.'

I learned that the French girl, would be in Greystones for a few more weeks. As Tramore was on the cards for my next port of call, I flexed my surfer muscles and asked, 'Hey, would you like to come on a day's surfing with me?'

She nodded vigorously, which I took to be an affirmative, and this permitted me to take details and say, 'au revoir' to Frances. While this was happening, Katherine was giggling and shaking her head in disapproval. Jurek gave a broad leer and mumbled under his breath, 'Well, Horse, (nickname) that's one trip you won't want me on!'

The Tramore day, dawned bright and sunny with a Force 5 south-westerly wind that would guarantee some swell getting into the Bay. I now had the beginning of a quiver of boards. These consisted of Rod Sumpter's light stringerless board, one heavy Bilbo, and the balsa board. Tramore was the target as most of us had been there before; I had as a kid, and reckoned it would be a good surfing venue. Furthermore, it was within easy reach of south County Dublin and I knew it had a beautiful south-facing beach. It had headlands on both ends, and for good measure the town spread up a steep hill and looked down on the splendid panorama, while supporting lots of sport-minded youth in its embrace. So, with the car loaded with boards, my 8mm movie camera and the French beach bunny, we headed south. We were going there with something to offer – boards and the prospects of joining a surf club. This was tempting stuff, and I wanted to sell the idea to the locals.

It must have looked really cool, our arriving with three prizes on top of the green station wagon, now plastered with surf decals. We parked midway down the prom at a wooden lifeguard hut and peered out to sea. Yep, there were nice summer waves – just right for learners. The beach was about three miles long, and on top of its headlands were large figures, each called the metal man, because there was a metal sailor on top of them, pointing to the rocks where ships could flounder. To the east side of the beach the land was flat but with some impressive dunes down the way.

Frances was delighted to see Tramore and said she would man the camera while I surfed, but added, 'Where are ze lifeguards?' We went to the railings and looked over to discover a bunch of guys sunbathing. There in front of our eyes were some of the future icons of Irish surfing. These were the guys, along with their buddies, who would carry the flag to many future surfing contests in far-off places. These were the surfers of Danann! They were very tanned, fit and healthy, so much so that Frances said, 'Are they Irish boys?'

I bore the insult because she was so cute, and mumbled, 'Of course.' The guys were sitting with backs against the sea wall, while beside them lay a fourteen-foot paddleboard – the sort we had used in the surf club stand at the Boat Show. I felt like a visitor from outer space as I hollered down at the boys,

'Would anyone like to surf on a real board'?

I used my very best beach boy drawl and held my breath. The effect was electric. Dave and Greg Kenny, both in chop-off jeans, jumped to their feet and swarmed up a rope that they had in lieu of a ladder. Behind them came Dave Griffin, Derek Musgrave and Eamon Matthews. Dave Kenny, who was called 'Dukie', later related:

'The first board I rode was our life-saving board similar to the old-fashioned Australian paddleboard, round to the nose and pointed at the stern, made of a hollow timber construction just like a boat and too heavy to bring out to the water's edge on my own. It was the lifeguard's rescue board. Now this guy Kevin Cavey had arrived with modern fibreglass boards that had fins! From then on all Irish surfing really happened and surfers began to get in contact with each other, and friendships were made that have lasted to this day. All this activity prompted me to get a subscription to Surfer magazine, which came out bi-monthly, which filled me and my friends in on what was going on in the rest of the surfing world.'

The Tramore lifeguards left to right; Hugh O'Brien Moran,
Willie Britton, Eamon Matthews and Paul Kenny.

With dedicated care, the boys helped unload the boards, stroking
them but saying nothing. Two of the boards were passed down
to the beach immediately. I followed while Frances manned the
camera. I used Sumpter's board for a demo and then passed it
over to egger hands. The wind was now quite reduced, the tide
was halfway in, and the waves were glassy and slow-breaking. In
moments, the beach four guards were to be seen riding to shore like
never before.

They each took turns at riding the glass boards and from their
performance it was clear that inside twenty minutes they had
already learned how to catch a wave and turn a board and cut
across the green walls. Frances was excited, shouting, 'I filmed all
those rides!' That pleased me, and to know she had caught Dave
Griffin in action.

Then it was time to get to know the boys. They all had younger
brothers who were expected down at the beach because word was
getting around. They were informed about the club, and they all

promised to join, and insisted that we return with the boards the following week. Dave Kenny said he would be studying in UCD for the winter, and while living in Dublin could even join the committee. I knew that would not present a problem, and Dave was as good as accepted on the spot. The question was raised as to where to buy boards. As a result, I signed up Dave Kenny for a ten-foot custom board, which would be delivered for the reduced price of £28. I also asked about who in the county council was responsible for supplying boards. It would be great for the guards to have some glass boards instead of the long wooden paddleboards that were so heavy to carry. As luck had it, eventually a sale was made, something that pleased the lifeguards. Our visit was heralded as a success and I returned as promised several times that summer, though Frances by then, had disappeared home to Paris.

Meeting these fellows was the beginning of another set of lifelong relationships that was also enhanced on my next visit, by the arrival of a band of younger brothers and friends. They had missed day one, but made sure to be there for my next visit. Greg Kenny was so fit that he was soon to become a PT instructor and a great surfer and windsurfer. Greg's younger brother, Paul, was ready on the beach on day two, and took to surfing from the first instance, becoming one of the best watermen that Tramore could offer. However, he was hard pressed by Derek Musgrave's brother Damien and one of Ireland's greatest surfers-to-be - Hugh O'Brien-Moran. Hugh, who had the physique of a Polynesian waterman and the dark colouring to go with it, was only about sixteen years old, but took to surfing like it was his destiny. Hugh was indeed a sort of Duke Kahanamoku in his own right.

Niall, who is Hugh's younger brother, was also highly motivated by the arrival of surfing on his shores. Along with Hugh, he immediately made plans to build a board from scratch. As it turned out, they produced so many glass boards that they began a rental business. To this day, Tramore has produced some of the strongest and most competitive surfers in the country. This explosion of talent took its genesis from that fateful summer's day in June 1966. Hugh later said:

'If you surfed a new spot then you could be sure it had never been surfed before. We started on the beaches, then gradually moved out to the reefs. I was involved in contest surfing for years, and travelled to European and World events. I still get out in the water if there's the slightest sign of surf. And I make trips to the west if the forecast is favourable. Wind and wave forecasts in recent times are so good you can surf world-class waves in Ireland, though usually only within a narrow window of time.'

Eamon Matthews gave us a reminder:

'My first surf on a glass/foam board was in Tramore around 1966, the board very kindly provided by your good self while the surf was typical summer two or three feet. I can still see, feel and hear the sensations as the board sliced across the little wave with the rail cutting blue water and the fin giving control as it held the tail. That was it, I was hooked! My first board by Northumbria was a disaster and best forgotten. It gave me nothing but frustration until I stripped the glass off and reshaped the blank into something that was lighter and better, if a little too 'mini' for me at the time.'

CHAPTER 8

The World Event in San Diego

This was an historic year for the progress of Irish surfing. Firstly, a club representing the whole island had been successfully formed. The club had then been publicly launched at the Irish Boat Show. Secondly, Roger Steadman had arrived in Ireland, and thirdly, Rodney Sumpter from Cornwall had visited. Now, to crown it all, the fourth factor was about to emerge.

The phone rang in Mount Herbert in or around the second week in September 1966.

'Haello, is Kevin Cavee there? This is Brennan McClelland calling from San Diego.'

Gulp. The lad's throat went dry and in a thin, high-pitched voice I squeaked, 'Yes this is he.'

'Well, Kevin, you will be pleased to know that we are inviting you to come to San Diego to compete in the World Surfing Championships in October. There are some Irish over here who want to meet you.'

My mind went into overdrive. Yes, it was true that I had pestered Pat McNulty for the past six months telling him all about surfing in Ireland, but I did not expect this result. Also, it was true that a dear older lady in Bray, Mrs Talbot Brady, had a brother in San Diego and he said he would see what he could do to get Ireland represented. She also had a relation who was Monsignor Joseph V. Clarkin of San Diego, who was likely to be an influential person, to say the least. It was also true that I was now having sleepless nights thinking about the great event that was about to happen, and how little chance I had of getting there. But I never expected such a fantastic offer, coming out of the blue and so close to the time of the event. It was miraculous!

For the remaining week, I was like a kid on hashish. I could not focus on anything and went wildly about getting gear together for the trip. As luck had it, the passport was in date and the benefactors – God bless them – sent the airline tickets by express mail. My work for my Dad went to zilch, and despite that I reckon that he knew it was pointless trying to snap me out of the dream.

It was then that the newspapers got hold of the story. The press carried two- or three-column pieces that had headings such as 'A young Irishman will compete in world surfing event'. The locals in Bray began to take notice. Someone said to my father, 'Bill, I hear your son is off to Miami to water ski.' Some said 'Acapulco' and many said they heard I was going swimming for Ireland. However, for others 'the dime dropped' and they realised what surfing was all about. It was something different and Ireland was about to have a share in this new-fangled foreign sport of Polynesian kings.

The main benefactors were Larry Gordon of Gordon & Smith Surfboards, along with Bob Seitz, who owned a Texaco garage, Laverne Walsh, a graphic artist, and both Dermot (Don) Foley and his business partner, Manuel Lira. They all lived in San Diego. The latter two fellows ran a dog parlour and Don was a brother of Mrs Talbot Brady in Bray. This was the connection that got the support of the Monsignor, who asked for sponsors from the pulpit. It appears his parishioners' extraordinary dedication directly contributed to the surf scene developing in Ireland. I was indebted to this group of people and made sure to visit them when time permitted.

I descended the steps of the aircraft, in San Diego to meet a tall middle-aged man with thinning hair and a boyish smile. He said he was Brennan McClelland, shook my hand and introduced his associate, Lee Strudevant, publicity director. Over the following days I met a host of faithful sponsors, including the aforementioned Larry Gordon, Laverne Walsh, Bob Seitz, Rev. Charles O'Connor of St John the Evangelist Catholic Church and Don Foley, who was one of the strongest supporters of the enterprise. Later I met Tom Gamble, one of Bob Ortman's sports columnists from the Evening Tribune and Pat McNulty, the editor of Surfer magazine who was preparing an article about the World event for the November edition of the Los Angeles Times supplement 'West'.

Then I met Dave McIntyre, who was to be the Ireland facilitator. He was a small guy with blond hair, decked in a blue-and-white hula shirt. He welcomed me with a firm handshake. Then he packed my baggage into a car and off we sped down a six-lane freeway fringed with tall phoenix palms. Dave McIntyre looked at me and said,

'Did you ever hear about the Duke?'

I nodded and said enthusiastically, 'Yeah, quite bit.'

Dave continued with a tone of reverence, relating what sounded like a well-rehearsed story:

'In 1890, he was born on Main Island in the Hawaiian archipelago. He was named Duke after the Duke of Edinburgh; would you believe that! His middle name was Paoa, a pure Hawaiian name. The family name was Kahanamoku, and they lived in the then unspoilt Waikiki Beach. By four years of age Duke had begun to surf and develop his aquatic skills. In 1912, he became an Olympic swimmer, while in 1924 he set a new world record in the 100-metre freestyle.'

Dave paused. Soon we turned off Cabrillo, and on to Rosecrans, continuing till we reached Shelter Island, which lay just short of Point Loma. Our destination was the magnificent Half Moon Inn that looked out over a romantic yacht harbour and marinas within the safe enclosure formed by Shelter Island itself. Across the road was the Tiki-Tiki restaurant that overlooked Coronado Island and which would be the competitors' early morning breakfast venue and briefing area at the start of each day's activities. The limo drew to a stop and I got out, stiff from travel and ready for a shower. I turned to Dave and thanked him for the interesting story about the Duke. Dave smiled and said,

'You know why I told you this; well, the reason is because you will meet him here tomorrow.'

Day One

At Dawn the following morning, I found myself breakfasting with teams and officials in the Tiki-Tiki restaurant. I suspected that Rodney Sumpter would be there representing the UK. True to expectations, I found Rod engulfed in a conversation about board-shaping and causing a stir as he did so. Rod said that, as he was representing Britain, he thought about putting a full Union Jack on his board, top and bottom. He had never seen anyone in Australia, France, Spain, East and West Coast USA and Hawaii ever paint a flag on a board. Finding a picture of the Union Jack was easy, but the taping up of each colour and keeping perfectly straight lines was not. Time and time again, he had ripped off the master tape to redo the lines. Finally, his red, white and blue weapon was ready for use in San Diego.

As I had not eaten the previous evening, the breakfast was most welcome, bacon with eggs sunny-side up and a hefty portion of hash browns. As the restaurant was on the second floor, with one side completely lined with glass, it commanded a spectacular view southward. Then their attention was drawn to Coronado Island, the naval air station and a silver-grey curve of land sweeping out to become the ominous Point Loma, dominating the bay. Chuck added,

'Coronado Island is where the Navy Seals become qualified. Camp Pendleton, up the coast, is where I will be going next month, as I am being drafted for Vietnam.'

The words caused a chill up my spine because not only did I think of Tom Casey's plight, but I thought it most difficult for a young man to give up such a wonderful life to fight a war. What a sacrifice! Then I realised just how poor a Marine I would have been if I had left home and attempted to enlist. At the table was one of the Hawaiian team members, Jock Sutherland, an infamous big-wave rider also George Greenough who said that if I was ever in Maraposa Lane, Santa Barbara, to call in and see him. Then the spell was broken by Brennan McClelland.

'Gu– Gu– Good mornin', competitors!'

A hundred youths bedecked in contestants' T-shirts turned in their seats and stared eagerly in his direction.

'Welcome to the third World Surfing Championships, organised by the International Surfing Federation and the United States Surfing Association. Incidentally, for those whom I have not had the pleasure of meeting yet, I'm the contest manager.'

He gave a big smile, and went on,

'This is day one, the one you've all been waiting for and reports are for small two- to three-foot surf, less than we had hoped for, but improving as we go down the week. We have invited Dale

Lawrence of the Scripps Institute to bring you up to date on the swell reports.'

With that a thin fellow in khaki Bermuda's and a white T-shirt addressed the group.

'We at Scripps get reports from the US Navy about the probability of swell heading this direction. The swell is evaluated by observance of special buoys that are anchored in the mid Pacific and close to California as well. As the buoys rise and drop between peaks and troughs they are timed. The period between each rise indicates the space between the waves. If they are spaced far apart it is from a distant storm and will most likely arrive here as large waves, and if close together are generated by more local winds. I'm glad to say that the aviation people have identified such a storm off the coast of Midway, and swell with long periods tracking this direction. We will have some pretty good waves by the middle of the week.'

Basically, that was his message and it was a good one. Brennan then carried on the briefing.

'We will depart in fifteen minutes, and the venue will be Mission Beach. For ease of transport, pack your boards into the trailer waiting outside and reclaim them at the beach.'

He added that this chosen beach was a secret as the San Diego school kids would like to know where we were today, as they would go AWOL to be there! Then he continued,

'We have some more very good news; the Ford motor company is bringing a new model out on the market. They are giving each team a brand new Camero convertible to use during the contest, so be careful.'

There was a very loud whoop from everyone, punctuated with 'Hee-haws' and whistles. The event was off to a very good start. Rod said, 'I'm sure you and I will be sharing that Camero with two other small teams, but we're going to have a wonderful time.' It was not long after this that Brennan announced that the cars were being taken from us all, because some bright sparks had driven theirs into the sea. What a shame!

La Jolla and Misssion Beach

As we arrived at the beach I got to meet some more icons of the sport; Midget Farrelly, Joey Cabell, Phyllis O'Donnell, Linda Benson, Wayne Cowper, George Downing who featured in my Sunset Beach mural, and of course Nat Young, who was now tipped to be a winner in the men's event. This third World Surfing Championships had as much to offer as the others, and probably more. It had magnificent water, sunny weather and an enthusiastic turnout of the greatest surfers from nine nations, all on view to an appreciative audience. Larry Gordon loaned me a magnificent pale green board for the duration of the event. Using the board I caught some small waves and it seems I impressed Margo Godfrey from the West Coast women's team. She egged me on by saying 'Go for it Kev!', 'Wow, nice ride!' and so on. I think she did it because I looked so unconfident and it was obvious that I needed encouragement. Margo eventually settled in Kauai and became a Christian Surfer.

The following day, because the waves had been poor in La Jolla, L.E. 'Hoppy' Swartz, the adjudicator, made the popular decision of moving the event to North Jetty, Mission Beach, a drive of one mile south. Once again, the contestants piled into the hospitality transport, that is after they had loaded their prized boards into trailer provided. With that, the surfing taskforce moved to the new location. When they arrived at the parking lot beside the beach, the Indian team representative, Jerry Bujakowski, yelled,

'Look d' the surf, it's beautiful, glassy and a decent size!'

Boards were unloaded, and the public-address system turned on. The judging desks were quickly set up, and the event continued as if nothing had happened – yet in much improved conditions. The surf at the jetty was about four feet, well-shaped and generally lefts, and there was every sign that Dale Lawrence's predictions would be correct. Nobody wore wetsuits though the air was chilly, but by 9am the sun burned off the early-morning mist and it got warm. It must have been the colour of the board that did the trick because I rode quite well. Though this was my first ever competition I caught two head high waves, and on both occasions dropped down the front, cranking a left turn, and then grabbing the outside rail of the board. This resulted in my riding high and tight across the wobbling walls of Pacific liquid. At the same time, I became partially covered by one as it tipped over. This scored me some badly needed points. I rode several other less challenging waves, but all points added gave me the points to qualify.

Rodney Sumpter takes up the story:

'The format for the 1966 World Surfing Championships in San Diego was three full surfing competitions back to back over seven days and when all the points were combined that give the winner. There were only three countries from Europe – Ireland, France and Great Britain – and they went along with Brazil and India to make up group two. All the countries were divided so there would be a group winner as well.

'Ireland rode in his first heat with Mike Doyle, and a host of others. Mike is well known for wearing the "Mike Doyle" large Lilliputian-style floppy hat. Ireland by now was getting used to the conditions and surfed the first day's heats well, coming third of six – enough to go through. Then again in the quarter-finals he caught enough waves with Irish determination and scraped through to the semi-finals where the stars of the contest – Steve Bigler, David Nuuhiwa, and Joey Cabell – were performing.'

The day had been so demanding that Rodney and several of us went to Joey Cabell's Charthouse restaurant for dinner. After we had placed our orders, we had a beer each. When the meal arrived, the whole table had fallen asleep – no exceptions! Later Rod assessed our progress:

'Kevin and I were both in the same heat but the waves were now getting tough to handle. Despite this uphill fight, we put up a good show as our boards often stood side by side, the emerald green and my Union Jack in red, white and blue – the brightest things in the contest.'

That evening, Laverne Walsh, one of the hostesses for the event, invited Bernard (Midget) Farrelly, Corky Carroll, Rodney and me to her home beside the beach at La Jolla. She made tea and we met her son, who was an ardent surfer, and were shown pictures of his surfing. Laverne showed us her computer-enhanced graphic art, as that was her business. This was an appropriate time to talk to Corky and Skip Fry, as they were relaxed and not distracted by the hubbub of the contest. Corky, as you can imagine, said he had Irish roots – the Carroll's of Co. Cork. Midget reckoned that his parents' families were originally from the south of England, and that kept Rodney happy.

Ocean Beach

The finals day was a Sunday, and a carnival atmosphere prevailed. Ocean Beach was the focus of ABC Television's Wide World of Sports, as is beamed out to millions of viewers nationwide. The onlookers were dressed for the occasion, and the attire ranged from 'bitsy' bikinis to cut-off denim shorts with pockets flapping or surfboard shorts; many wore planter-style straw hats and some wore Stetsons. The crowd lined the beach and pier, frequently cheering at the exciting display.

As an added attraction, some of the women surfers paddled out beyond the pier and out of the contest area. They intended getting in some practice before the next heat. Joyce Hoffman was seen lining up to ride a gigantic set of waves, the biggest that day. She picked the highest peak, and after several strokes came flashing down its face. Her lean silhouette could be seen, with feet wide apart, nimbly working the board in arcs and turns, across the spilling wave. Joyce's surfing standard seemed equal to, if not better than the best of male surfers on that day. I suspected that if she had been in the male event, the ride would have earned her the highest marks of the contest. Right after that the women's finals were run, and true to form, Joyce Hoffman was the winner. The other Nai'a (dolphins) also surfed aggressively and took some magnificent rides.

The crowd were impressed, and the day was enhanced by an Australian-style dory race. There was also an exciting demonstration of catamaran surfing by Hobie Alter in his Hobie Cat. The display became even more exciting when, despite Hobie's skill, his catamaran got hit from the side by a wave, throwing both the crew and loads of sailing paraphernalia into the water. The crowd loved it! Just then the PA blared, 'Will the competitors for the semi-finals please line up on the beach!'

This was to be a crowning moment for Ireland as the cameras rolled and ABC got on the air. Then with a flurry the eight-man heat entered the water. The waves were a good head-high but slow. I had been seeded through to this semi-final, as was India. It was probably good PR for the sport to have some new nations seen on TV. They also knew that neither of us would pose a threat to the finalists. I noticed that Jerry Bujakowski who had been wearing runners in earlier events had grown wise and scotched the idea for the semis. It was thrilling to paddle out wearing a green vest, on a green board and to be partially in the battle for supremacy in the waves fought out by the sons and daughters of past Gods of the sea. Rodney was already whipping all over the place, and Jock Sutherland was nose-riding while standing backwards.

Corky and Skip were doing wide-bottom turns and Steve Bigler was doing the same, but let his arm swing in a theatrical type of gesture, each time he dropped in. Jerry Bujakowski was much like me, floundering around and only picking up scrappy rides. Suddenly there were only moments left to go and a nice-looking wave appeared, I thought maybe this will be my salvation. Just then the horn went to signal end of semis. Then, to make matters worse, out of the kindness of his heart, Pat McNulty announced:

'This next wave will count for Ireland.'

All eyes turned to watch the green-clad figure on a green board, thinking that he was about to explode into action at any moment. The wave hovered over my head. I paddled like I had never paddled before, but with a roar and jerk, my nosedived, I stalled and the wave passed by. No more need be said!

Rodney Sumpter competes in the 1966 World event while riding his Union Jack embellished board. Also, the winning ride by Nat Young of Australia

Now, as the men's finals began with six brawny Kekoa (warriors) paddled out to begin their amphibious warfare. At this stage, the waves had even gotten larger and so the rides were more exciting. The eventual winner of this event was Nat Young from Australian with 293 points, followed by Jock Sutherland the Hawaiian with 230, while fifth was Rodney Sumpter with 182 points. Cameras rolled and ABC began to chatter the news around the USA. Rod's coming fifth in the main individual event was cream on the cake, and capped his six-year-old surfing career. This was an amazing feat, considering the competition of seventy surfers from twenty-one countries. He was also proud to be group winner and later received a huge trophy, two feet high, made from marble and redwood and shaped like the state of California. The Hawaiian team, which included Jock Sutherland was headed by the great Duke Kahanmoku, was a favourite to win the team event, and that's just what they did. Nat Young became the outright contest winner because he seemed to execute simple, yet functional turns, expressed in an individual way. Nat had demonstrated a style of surfing that would lead to a worldwide reduction in the length of boards. His much more functional surfing style clocked up scores, clearly illustrating the changing mood in surfing – the transformation from classical nose riding on long boards to complete freedom of movement on much smaller boards. The final results of the Men's Competition: Nat Young, Australia, 293 pts - Jock Sutherland, Hawaii, 230 pts - Corky Carroll, West Coast USA, 223 pts - Steve Bigler, West Coast USA, 223 pts - Rodney Sumpter, England, 182 pts - Bernard (Midget) Farrelly, Australia, 171 pts

The final results of the Women's Competition: Joyce Hoffman, West Coast USA, 86 pts - Joey Hanaski, West Coast USA, 70 pts - Mimi Munro, East Coast USA, 64 pts -Gail Cooper, Australia, 64 pts - Josette Lagardare, West Coast USA, 50 pts - Phyllis O'Donnell, Australia, 46 pts

Meet the Master

The Duke, then seventy-six years of age, presented the prizes on the beach, and remarked how surfing has developed into a great sport that now ranked with any in the world. With the contest now completed. At the farewell 'Luau' that evening, just as Dave McIntyre had predicted, the teams got to meet the famous Duke. His arrival was heralded by some excitement as the organisers had forgotten to set a place for him, and the oversight had to be rectified. When he made a speech the ovation afterwards lasted ten minutes, and when the Luau was over contestants were invited to line up to meet the icon. When it was Ireland's turn, I approached the Duke, who was standing tall and erect and wearing a navy blazer and white pants. His skin was mahogany brown and his white hair was swept back. When I told, where I was from, he closed his eyes as if recollecting, and said with his eyes still closed, 'Ah! Ireland.' I thought for a moment he had heard about our surfing? But, alas he said,

'I would love to go there and golf.'

The next day we all said our goodbyes and departed, thrilled by the experience and thankful for having the honour of meeting the Duke. Now I was invigorated like never before, as the next challenge would definitely be to hold a surfing championship in Ireland – why not!

I had to pay respects to Don Foley my main benefactor. I went to visit his home when I got to his house on Poinsettia Drive, I noticed a tattered Irish flag flying on a mast in his front lawn. Don was proud of his heritage and hoped I had scored some high points in the contest. As luck had it, I was able to present Don with a brand-new tricolour brought from Ireland and thank him and Manuel for all that they did.

CHAPTER 9

The Boards of Antrim

When I returned from San Diego, the club members were excited to hear how it had gone. I described the event and we discussed how it was run, and it became apparent that we could do the same. This idea was met with the nodding of heads and unanimous agreement. Also, the boys up north had been advancing in leaps and bounds. There was a letter from Bo Vance that he had now made contact with Davy Govan and Alan Duke. At the same time Martin Lloyd, a friend of theirs, mailed a card showing their surfing adventures in Rossbeg, Co. Donegal, where they got some incredibly long rides. They were riding right, while crossing the mouth of one bay and riding into another. Martin sent a map and pictures.

Bo remembers the time well as he had also been present:

'I met Martin Lloyd in the mid Sixties when we worked for the same Belfast electronics company and shared an interest in mountaineering. Alistair ('Mac') McCartney, who followed us into surfing, also loved the mountains. My elder brother, Mason, kept a caravan in Donegal and returned from a holiday there most enthusiastic about having met another Belfast family on the beach and having tried their belly-boards. When I joined them on the next trip I really enjoyed that exhilarating sport.'

'Now, wondering if real surfboards would work in our small waves, we scaled up drawings of a Hawaiian board (ten feet by two foot) which we found in an old water sports book, and using these, shaped a polystyrene block. Fortunately, the drawings indicated a rocker or curve. A friend covered the polystyrene with chopped strand mat and polyester resin, not knowing that that would dissolve the polystyrene. It was a disaster! Apart from the rough finish the core had shrunk and was loose inside the skin. It was tried out in Donegal and impressed a farmer who said, "Ye can swim out t'sea an' git washed shorewards again!"

'Cracks appeared in the board so I glassed in a metal valve at the tail and by pumping it up before use, it became watertight. At least we knew that surfing here would be possible. Then in an effort to protect a new core we wallpapered it and varnished the paper before glassing. This was a remarkable success and several serviceable boards were made this way. We were now glassing them ourselves, using woven cloth instead of chopped strand mat, and had no problem with resin reaching the core. We were now modernising our shapes and our boards were now from eight to eleven feet long with a three-inch rocker, round tails and large plywood fins. By this stage we had learned about Kevin Cavey's efforts to promote the sport and through him learned about Davie Govan, Alan Duke and Ted Alexander [Bangor], who had now got their boards from Bilbo. This meant that we could now see how boards should be shaped.'

Alan Duke, Clive Davies and Martin Lloyd work on
one of their first homemade fibreglass boards

'Then Martin Lloyd located a supplier of single-skin, unlined neoprene, making it possible for us to make cheap, comfortable wetsuits. In order that they would not tear when being put on, we had to dust them with Johnson's baby talc. Then, in a stroke of genius, a friend told us to use epoxy resin as it would not dissolve the polystyrene. We now had a light yet strong construction which put us at least ten years ahead of the world, though we did not know it at the time!'

Bo Vance also told us how his boys analysed the swell reports.

'We found we could get accurate weather forecasts direct from Aldergrove Met Office and as we grew to know the staff there we learned about three weather ships, India, Juliet and Kilo, out in the Atlantic. These ships sent sea condition reports every six hours, coded in six-digit numbers which we learned to decode. Each day we phoned Aldergrove, got the latest three numbers and decoded these to give swell height, direction and wave period at three locations. Since wave period determines the speed of the wave we could calculate when waves heading our way should arrive. We got quite excited when periods of ten seconds or more were reported, especially with the larger swells, as this meant a chance of fast, powerful waves. All this stuff was plotted on tables and maps photocopied for the purpose, with a new issue each week. The system was far from perfect but did give some useful information and of course sometimes saved a long drive to find a flat calm!'

So, bearing Bo's advice in mind, we got more geophysical, and began to analyse the weather forecasts with more accuracy. Not long after that Bo came south and met four of the club. We showed him around the east coast beaches and settled on surfing the north end of the Brittas Bay – the best of a bad lot at that time. Over a pint at McDaniel's, Bo gave us more information about their activities:

'We are building fond memories already. You see, small groups of us camp at, perhaps, Rosbeg, and wait for swell that often comes with the evening tide, serenaded with the Beach Boys' numbers by the guitars of Martin or Davie, who you have already met. Davie and I took a van to Cornwall recently and bought as many new and used boards as we could stack on the van. These and a few more that Bilbo sold us at a hefty discount are now being spread around the folk on the north coast. Despite that the old troopers continue to make improved versions of their boards and wetsuits, thus keeping cost to a minimum.'

Aughris Quay

Soon, filled with renewed spirit of adventure Roger, Jurek, Colm and Pat Kinsella set off to Sligo. Pat was now a new man, as his exam was over, and he had forgiven us for the earlier rough treatment. Already we missed Tom Casey for his humour, who by now should be somewhere over the Mekong Delta singing 'The Mayor of Bayswater' and maybe missing our Irish banter.

As usual, the winter weather was foul and the sea was enormous. Therefore, we consulted the Ordnance Survey map to locate somewhere with a beach and shelter. Aughris Head, just south-west of Strandhill, looked like the place. We had previously gone north of Sligo, but this time we would go south and west towards Mayo. We therefore wheeled left at Ballisodare, where the beautiful white swans always used to swim in the river, turned south, and bounced over twisted roads keeping Donegal Bay on our right and leprechaun-type hills to our left – but also noticing Carrowkeel was fading out behind us. Carrowkeel is one of hundreds of mountaintop graves that are characteristic of Sligo. It is a megalithic monument and burial site embedded under heaps of rock, and situated high in the hills. We spied Aughris head and also saw a sign for Aughris Quay. We turned right at Battles grocery store and headed along a narrow road till we emerged high above a amall concrete boat slip. Though visibility was poor, we could see waves passing by on their way to shore. We reckoned that no surfer had yet trod this path. So, without a thought we said,

'Let's get in, there is supposed to be a beach inside – let's try for it!'

In moments, I had paddled out into the swell that now looked huge. I looked for the others but they had not followed. Now there were two choices: either struggle back to the disappearing slip or surf into shore. Therefore, I choose the latter, and began to scratch hard to get on any wave that came. All I wanted was a big broken wall that would catapult me inwards and I would climb up and ride the white water. To catch a huge green wall in a howling wind was not an easy matter. This was very different from the tropics; it was loaded with spooks. Then an extra-large set came through and it began a very slow peel just before arriving. I was miraculously pushed forward and instantly stood and was hurled towards shore and the unknown. The boys said that they snatched a photo as the wave tipped over and I disappeared into the mist. Then they bundled into the car and discovered a lane that we had previously passed, and it took them directly to the envisaged beach. To their relief or entertainment, I was there, dragging in my board and shouting, 'Did ya see that?'

Of course, no one did see anything but they had now found a nice new strand. Roger already in wetsuit, ploughed out to catch the nice re-forming inside breaks, riding lefts or rights and sometimes both at a time. Then to our joy we discovered that, like any good beach area, it had a pub. This was a whitewashed cottage with a sign 'Bar' over the door. It looked so quaint that we posed for a photo for posterity. When we went inside we discovered a small and unadorned counter and a turf fire. At that time, the counter was on left side of the room and, what's more, there was immediate service. I was permitted to take off my wetsuit and dress in the pub, and this also became a habit for future visits.

After about an hour a small man who was drinking at the counter put down his glass and stood on a chair and said, 'Would someone mind moving their car as 'me van' is blocked and I have to make a delivery.'

Someone immediately obliged and he delivered his crates of Coca-Cola; a bit late, but at least he got the right day!

Kerry Wedding

An old friend, Jurg Kuhn, from Zurich, (as opposed to Jurek from Bray) arrived in Kerry to work as a chef in Ard na Sidhe hotel at Caragh Lake. He proposed to a pretty Kerry rose called Margaret who worked in the Europe Hotel. I was honoured to be their best man, and prepared to perform the many duties it entailed as long as I could also get in a Co. Kerry Surf. The day before the wedding I headed to Waterville and while driving through the town, noticed some nicely shaped waves breaking at the mouth of the river that flows out from the adjoining Lough Curran. I had to make my way through private land, till I finally got to the hard-packed bed of the river mouth. I pushed my precious Sumpter board outwards while all the time feeling for rocks with my feet and secretly dreading the snapping of some unknown undersea creature, that only Kerry could produce! Then, quite satisfied about safety, I mounted the board and paddled for the first approaching wall. It was about waist high, as waves often are. I picked it up after several strokes and rode the first of many nice lefts that day. Glad to say, there were no underwater surprises or even the threat of a farmer with a gun.

Then I ventured on towards Derrynane, but while high up on the cliff road spied some waves breaking very far below. I reckoned I might be the only person ever to bother struggling down there, and therefore proceeded to slide my board through almost vertical fields, one after another, till I eventually staggered on to the beach. I rode some chest-high breaks for about a half an hour, and then faced a return trip back up through the steep patchwork of meadows and walls. Though exhausted by the experience I felt it was a job well done. That was purely my opinion, of course; I knew I had proved absolutely nothing. However, it is likely that most surfers over the years will ever give that beach a second thought.

Members and Associates

At the next meeting of the Club the National Contest was the main item for discussion. However firstly it was proposed that the club name should be changed to 'Surf Club of Ireland'. It was accepted, because it was less east-coast orientated and therefore more accommodating for members living in other counties. Next, we needed a census of members and associates, though few ever paid a club fee. Many were just well-wishers and people tied by an invisible bond of mutual understanding and the spirit of adventure:

From Dublin and Wicklow there was Roger Steadman, Harry Evans, Tony Gleeson, Dermot Hughes, Pat Kinsella, Eric Fox, Rodney Touch, Willie Hurst, Dermot Herlihy, Susan Fawcett and Johnny Lee.

From Co. Cork there was Jane Cross, Tom Flynn, Sean O'Connell, Kevin Nagel, Frank McEnnis, along with Tom O'Brien and his brother. Tom could not hear nor speak from birth and uses a notebook to this day to convey his thoughts, to which one writes a reply. This method is slow but very effective as no one misses out on what the other is saying.

From Co. Sligo there was In Willie Parks, Jean Parks, Helena Condon, with two very young lads at the time, Stan Burns, Tom Hickey, both of whom would soon become icons of the sport, giving it time and devotion.

From Co. Clare there was Eddie Comber, Pip Cullen, Hugh Milne, Mike Murphy, Brian Cusack and Wally Fogarty, Sam McCrum, John Guinan and Antoin O'Looney, who was photographed riding on a fifteen-foot face in Lahinch. Later, Antoin was given an award for paddling a ten-foot board across the English Channel for a charity.

From Co. Donegal there was Brian Britton, along with his four brothers, Kevin McCloskey, Grant Robinson, and Ted Alexander who was from Bangor, but now stayed in Rossnowlagh.

From Co. Antrim there was Desmond, Bo Vance, Ian Hill, Alan Duke, Davie Govan, Olly Pierce, Charlie Adjey, and Martin Lloyd, and Alan Duke.

From Co. Waterford there was Dave, Greg and Paul Kenny, Michael Counihan, Eamon Matthews, Dave Griffin, Derek and Damien Musgrave, Justin O'Mahony, Dick Power, Mark Kelleher and Philip Sherry. In addition to this young blood, there was another asset – their parents, who in their own way had influence in town affairs. One of these was Doctor Quain, a pal of Doctor O'Brien-Moran who was the father of Hugh, Niall and three others. These two medical 'Daddios' both bought boards from C&S. Doc Quain was the envy of the community because he laced out £50 to buy an all-black board, the likes of which had never been seen before!

Bearing all this in mind, it was now time to discuss the $64,000 question: Could we run a contest in Ireland and where would it be held? There was no opposition to the questions, only enthusiastic agreement. So, running a contest was put forward as a proposal and passed unanimously.

Then there was a burst of conversation followed by Roger saying,

'I think we have made the right decision, and now we have yet to figure out where to run it.' Then he held up the long list of members and said, 'Let's review our position.'

Now Harry Evans showed his mettle by pointing at the end of the list of members and stating his opinion:

'Wherever we hold the contest, we will have to work yet rely on local assistance. This means the most reasonable venue should have surf, accommodation, and proximity to rail, sea and air and a bunch of local enthusiasts. Now, so far Tramore bears all those hallmarks.'

People nodded in agreement and, as a result, Dave Kenny was asked if he thought Tramore would take the event. Dave, who had been keeping quiet, spoke up with conviction: 'Yes, they will. I will make sure of that!'

Nobody doubted his word, and September 3rd, 1967 became our planned D-Day! At that time Tramore was where most of the surfers were based. It was also where we knew we would be welcomed with open arms and with enthusiasm. Tramore's first asset was accommodation. There were plenty of B&BS and two fine hotels in which we could have an awards banquet to conclude the event. We got word from Cornwall that Rodney Sumpter was prepared to come over to our event, and would try and rally some others. We therefore expanded the event to include an international section. This was agreed but Dave Kenny questioned,

'Where will they stay, how many will come, and who will pay?

Roger piped up,

'Kevin has a good contact in Pepsi Cola through his Dad's hotel and feels sure he could get the event sponsored.' He added,'

The sponsorship will hopefully cover accommodation, admin for the event and hospitality, if all goes as planned. I reckon we will get about a dozen internationals at maximum and that's a manageable number.'

This generosity would become a trademark of Irish contests – a little touch of class that many other contests did not provide. Pepsi Cola agreed to sponsor the event and printed scoring cards designed from samples brought from San Diego.

Rodney Sumpter remembers how he drummed up interest in the Tramore contest:

'Out in the big blue yonder of Cornwall, there had been a buzz of activity about the Irish event. A year had passed since the World in San Diego. Nat Young's influence had everyone looking for a board with more speed to turn, and that would hold into the curl, tube ride and handle any conditions. Thus, started the biggest movement in surfing; the race for the perfect board was on. In Britain, as you know, I was shaping for Bilbo surfboards, the biggest surfboard builders in Europe. Kevin and Roger Steadman, had formed C&S Surfboards and were now ordering lots of boards to keep up with the ever-increasing demand. Each board had my personal signature written on the stringer while on the nose we placed a special decal in the shape of a shamrock with C&S written on the leaves. When Kevin's letter arrived for me at the Bilbo shop, Newquay, inviting me to the event, I in turn thought, why not get as many surfers as I could find. Then he told me it had been upped to include an International Championships – this then became a must-do trip!'

'This was ground-breaking news, and as I was ever keen to go, I wrote back accepting the invitation. At first, I could only rally six surfers, but a week before the contest I had managed to secure twelve able-bodied volunteers. I did this by saying, this is the chance of a lifetime, there may never be another Irish contest or it may be the first of many; either way, we see the island, ride some waves, and make history while we go! With that I secured my brother, Dave, Johnny McIlroy, Chris Kennings, Tigger Newling, James Trout, John Baxendale, Des Thomas, Nick Kavanagh, several pals and of course myself. There was a fellow called Alan Rich from California who said he just might wander over later.'

Looking at Rod's list, I recall that Tigger Newling was quite famous though still a youth. He was from Treymon Bay where in the Sixties his parents bought a house and they all became part of the British surfing scene. Tigger came into his own when short boards came into fashion. This permitted him to be daring and a lot more radical than most. Tigger said that designing and making boards in the beginning was the only way he could stay in the sport. He eventually began to sell boards under the name of Tig Surfboards, yet despite this achievement his ambition was to get to Australia.

I also had a detailed letter from John Baxendale and Des Thompson about their endeavours. They were based on the Lleyn Peninsula. They formed a club called the North East West Surf Club, and proceeded to make boards under the name of Northumbria. This was to support the club's expansion. C&S bought some of their boards and sold them on to ambitious surfers who wanted something other than Bilbo. John and Des later joined us on a surfari to Sligo, where we surfed in storm conditions close to the headland west of Dutchman's. That day the sea was so wild that Aughris or this bay provided the only shelter.

CHAPTER 10

First Irish Surfing Championships, September 1967

Just before the Tramore event, I took delivery of my latest board: another ten-foot Bilbo board designed by Rodney. It was bright yellow and had a flat underside to the front because it was promoted as a nose rider. True to its name, I found it really did allow me to hang five with ease. This board was to bring me some temporary success at the forthcoming contest.

Just a few days before September 1st, Tigger Newling, James Trout and Nick Kavanagh arrived at Mount Herbert – my folks' house in Bray, and stayed the night. Next morning, they were photographed in front of the house, just before heading for Tramore. Jenny was a Spanish student staying in our house to learn English so I told her she could come along. I loaded up and followed them so as to begin setting up for the event.

On our arrival in Tramore I shuddered to notice how small the waves appeared, but knew that a storm was in the making, and it should help. As arranged, the Tramore Fáilte brought us a caravan to place on the seafront for judging purposes, and they also provided a P.A. system. By September 2nd the rest of the Internationals arrived, to be greeted by wet weather and lots of friendly but curious Tramore surfers in the making. Rod Sumpter introduced people to people and, as you can imagine, it was a matter of getting grub, then dish out the accommodation and straight into the pub along with the older Tramore surfers and our committee.

By 9 p.m. everyone was in great form and ready to meet Dr O'Brien-Moran, who was the patron of the town in every sense of the word. He demonstrated his talent for oratory by giving them an introduction to the town's history, and thus put an official spin on the evening. The visitors also met other surfers from the four corners of the island, rolled their cigarettes, told tall yarns, and enjoyed the local brew. I was concerned about the lack of waves, but still hopeful for that southerly wind that now appeared to be building by the hour. To find that out I had to make frequent trips to the sea wall in the rain, but it was all a sweet encounter. The surf had been no more than a foot that afternoon, but by 10 p.m. it had increased I speculated while staring into the darkness! I brought this false news to the pub, and it helped raise the cheer.

The morning of September 3rd started with a surf check at first light. The wind had turned more westerly and the waves were still very small but there was a chance of an improvement as the tide pushed in. The lifeguard hut was now decorated and the judging caravan had been sited beside it. We had competition T-shirts with 'Pepsi Cola Surfing Event' written in red. Harry and Roger both wore one to set the trend. I was voted Competition Manager, while Harry was scoring auditor along with a willing member called P.J. Clearihan from Lahinch. Roger took over registration of up to twenty-eight competitors and Dave, along with several Tramore fellows, took club memberships, performed crowd control, and acted as beach marshals. Vivienne, Harry's daughter, was detailed to try and find some female competitors, but Jane Cross had not arrived from Cork and she felt a bit isolated.

It was decided to stall the event for a while, and wait on the rising tide.

When the P.A. system warmed up, I began to say nice things about the coming event, which caused some people to gather. All the time

Roger was very busy getting more and more competitors, added to by the late arrival of the Internationals, some fresh out of the sack. Just then a smiling freckle-faced fellow with dark curly hair, jeans and a black zip-up sweater approached Roger and me as we were changing for the first of the heats. Around his neck was a large Nikon camera with an 800mm lens at the ready.

'Hi, I'm Alan Rich. I'm from California,' he said with a grin.

'Is there an event on here? Rod Sumpter said there would be.'

'Wow!' Roger retorted. 'Do you surf? We have an international competition and it's open to everyone.'

'That's great, if I can borrow a board, I will enter'

'Good, we will fix you up, and now we can add USA to our list.'

As it turned out Alan was a surf photographer, knew Pat McNulty and later wrote a two-page spread about the contest for Surfer magazine that helped put us on the map. **(1)**

Alan borrowed a board and went out for a trial surf.

Rod said, 'Alan was riding a fast 9' 8" with balsa stringer and soft neutral rail. Despite the small waves, he looked like he was the man to beat. He rode with all the style of a Californian hottie.'

Rod thought Alan surfed well, and later they shared their photographic knowledge. Rod had brought his 16mm Rolex and enough film for a sequence in a movie he intended to make. I got to speak on the intercom about the event, making excuses about the lack of good waves. Then to keep the show on the road I sang from a commercial 'Things go better with Coca Cola, things go better with Coke'. There was a thump on the caravan window and one of the guys yelled, 'Pepsi not Coke!' Oops, wrong cola.

As the tide rose the wind turned onshore and miraculously pushed the waves to shoulder high. This direction meant that the waves would be sloppy but at least rideable. At 1 p.m. an announcement was made:

'We are pleased to say that the contest will now begin.'

There was a cheer and at that moment a Celtic pipe band marched down the promenade as if it were part of the event. This drew an enormous crowd and Alan took photos and began to record the incident. The beach marshals swung into action and lined up the six competitors for the first ever surfing competition to enter the water in Ireland. Looking back, the event was quite unique as none of the competitors wore wetsuits, just white T-shirts with numbers. Dave Kenny shouted out the competitor's rules of engagement to the contestants:

'You will get ten points for a good stand-up ride, with good distance and some fast turns, and less for a poorer performance. Therefore, taking today's conditions, on average most people will get two's and three's. You will be marked on your five highest rides and have twenty minutes to perform. There are four judges, three of which are from Cornwall. They have heat cards and will mark what they think you deserve, and these scores are averaged so the three highest go through to the quarter finals.'

They nodded and a whistle blew. To this day, that is basically all that happens in a surf contest, bar a few refinements depending on conditions or standard of event. Some of those in the first heat just pushed their boards beyond the break and turned them back towards shore, then jumped up and glided inwards to gain a few valuable points. Dave Griffin, Wally Fogarty and Pat Kinsella were part of the first heat. Dave and Pat were seeded to the next level, having put up the best performance. Gradually the tide rose above the three-quarter mark and, as expected, the waves again increased in size. Finally, as the sea hit the prom the backwash pushed the waves up to about four feet. At this stage, it was difficult for novices to get out beyond the break, paving the way for the more experienced dudes like Hugh O'Brien-Moran, Des Vance, Eamon Matthews, Derek Musgrave, Roger and myself to get in the finals. I won the event and was presented with a copper wave created by Fergus O'Farrell, the Celtic crafts designer in Dublin. (2)

One of the guys explained the best surfing tactics under those conditions:

'I managed to get outside quite quickly and caught a strong wave. The trick in those days was not to fall off, as no one had a leash. As luck had it, I rode the wave to shore and because of intense drag did not try to paddle out against it, but got out and ran up the beach opposite the current. Then I paddled back with the current and out to about the same place as before. I repeated that three more times and that way managed to well in the competition.'

Roger was a very close second, Martin Lloyd was third, Dave Kenny was fourth but not last, as there were a fifth and sixth whose names were not correctly recorded, but most likely Eamon Matthews and Bo Vance. That night the pub was the place to meet. Alan wrote of many aspects of the contest but he also mentioned that on the second night's party in one of the bars 'Jenny danced'. Now, not many people understood what it meant, but here it is. This was Jenny from Spain, who was an au pair girl from Bray, and whom we had persuaded to come for the event. I had brought the Hawaiian grass skirt, for the laugh, but did not know who might ever wear it. So I gave it to Jenny the Spanish girl, and to everyone's delight she just got up there and began to hula dance. The crowd laughed and applauded and so did the customers, who had never seen anything so alien in their local. We all gave full marks to Jenny for her courage.

(1) Alan's article was in the February 1968 edition of Surfer Magazine Page 72 and 73.

(2) In 2007, the Copper Wave was donated to T Bay S. C.

The Finals

By the following day, Sunday 3rd September, the waves had grown to storm proportions. Peaks were a good five feet as the International competitors entered the sea. The crowds had now grown in anticipation, and were rewarded as the standard of surfing was absolutely enthralling. Fellows were dropping in on waves that none of us locals would have tackled, at least not till the next day. The Cornish demons walked to the nose of their boards, hung ten like the pictures you see from California or Australia, and then moved back to whip their boards in another direction. A fellow called Johnny Mac (or 'Animal' as he was known) did some graphic loops and twirls while hanging on to his board like he was glued to it.

Tigger Newling and Alan Rich were tough competition for Rod. Undaunted, Rod threw in a few tricks, not only to gain points but to impress the audience. He would knee-paddle outside, turn his board with tail towards land and paddle for the next wave, just like he had done for us in Brittas Bay. The result was that as his board came down the face of the swell, the fin would bite and his board would do a 360-degree turn. His next thrill was to stand on his head at the most critical part of a take-off, and then sit down for the remainder of the ride. Needless to say, Rod won the day. He was fifth in San Diego and now an easy first in Ireland. Alan Rich got a good second and then continued photographing the activities. Roger took the mike and gave a vivid commentary on the event:

'We are witnessing today a great moment for Irish surfing history, and one that will never be forgotten.'

Eamon Matthews looks back to that time:

'The first Irish Championships in 1967 was indeed exciting and quite an organisational achievement by Kevin and Roger. I managed to finish in second place between the two of them in those gale-driven onshore conditions. I commenced college that September, little realising that I was also to commence that life-long battle of trying to balance work with my aquatic interests. I have little recollection of later contests other than coming second in three National Championships. I believe the last of these was in 1983. My attitude to surf contests became rather ambivalent until the very late Seventies when under the influence of Paul Kenny and Hugh, it began to seem like fun again. The other factor would have been the progression of contests from mediocre beach conditions to the reefs, where wave quality and power were so much more interesting.'

Celtic Luau

It was time to retire and present the prizes, and time for an Irish-style Luau. We didn't have a Duke Kahanamouku or a King Kahmeahmea, but we needn't have worried, because we had a perfect substitute in Dr O'Brien-Moran. There was no international icon present, and yet everyone present was an icon in the making. These blokes and girls, all adventurers and enthusiasts, were chips from the same spiritual block that inspired the ancient Hawaiians.

Humming with these thoughts and the satisfaction of riding the salty ocean, we all went as planned to the Grand Hotel on the hill and gathered in the bar. There were thirty of us – competitors who had not yet gone home, the visitors from Cornwall, the representative from Pepsi Cola and, most important, the Doc. The excitement of the two days was still lingering in the air. Someone said we had done the good thing and invoked the gods of the sea. This time round it was not to be the Hawaiian god Akua but a Celtic god called Manannan who might, if we were respectful, be at our beck and call, and give us clean oceans filled with the energy from paradise!

I too, was in a heavenly mood, and wearing an Oxford button-down – just like the kids from La Jolla. It was time to splurge, so Roger and I had a Cork dry gin and tonic, and I puffed on a Gauloises cigarette; I never inhaled – I just liked the perfume. Harry said that we were about to conclude an historic event. With that, we went into the function room and sat at a U-shaped table.

I declined the idea of a head table, so everyone just sat where they pleased, though I knew that while this informality was golden, the ethos could not survive; in future others might prefer to demonstrate status. But it worked well that evening.

SURFING AT TRAMORE

The finalists in the Irish National Surfing Championship at Tramore on Sunday last: K. Cavey (Bray), M. Lloyd (Belfast), R. Steadman (Bray) and E. Matthews (Tramore).

Competitors battling their way through the breakers.

Contest Winners, the Author, Martin Lloyd,
Roger Steadman and Eamon Matthews.

We dined on the most competitively priced menu of soup, roast chicken, mushy peas, mashed potatoes and sherry trifle, all of which cost the sponsors twelve shillings per person. This was simple food, and good value, and everyone was satisfied. As floral-patterned shirts were difficult to get in those days many of the surfers just wore heavy jumpers and saved time in the mornings by wearing scruffy beards or bearing dark blue shadow. The trophies were handed out by the representative from Pepsi Cola, who had forgiven me for my earlier blunder.

With the event concluded, people went their way, or stayed the night. Next day Tigger Newling, Rod and several Cornish blokes were to head down the south coast towards Kerry and hoped to reach Barley Cove in the extreme south-west. As some of us islanders still had a day free, we tagged along in the beginning and led them towards Annestown, but stopped short of Bunmahon and turned down a lane that led to a cliff and a rocky inlet called Benmoy. As the cliffs were low and grassy we managed to slide down quite easily and paddled out into some small, well-shaped surf.

The best ride of the day was taken by Alan Rich, who used my stringerless board to whip his way all over a few waist-high walls. Then we gathered for a group photo in which there were both Rod and David, his brother, as well as Roger, Harry, Johnny Lee, Ted Alexander and a host of others. This tiny cove close to Tramore was to be the launching pad for the first-ever visitors' surfari. So as the sun rose high on the glassy ocean our groups separated – the locals heading home and the visitors heading south. Rodney takes up the story:

The January Surfari

As usual, I had to work in the hotel over Christmas. By January 1st, 1968 I could not wait to get away on surfari to anywhere. After being indoors for several weeks the cold did not matter – in fact, it was very welcome.

Dave Kenny, Ken McCabe, Johnny Lee and myself, all with our wives or girlfriends, decided on going to Strandhill, the beach where our first surfari had landed in '66. We all checked in to the Baymount Hotel, and once again jested with the owner, Mr Byrne, who remembered us from before. It was nasty weather with heavy snow on the hills. The sea was very big and as a result no one wanted to get in. However, Dave said, 'Let's get decked out and just ride the white water. 'Ken and Johnny both grunted, 'You're mad!' I agreed that he was mad, but also agreed to get in. We both went hesitantly to the edge of the roaring Atlantic and peered out. Then we got in and began to paddle out just a little. Then it seemed like a sort of lull came about, so with nothing to stop us we took advantage of the calm and kept paddling outwards. We did not understand the lull. It was as if we were between sets, and it was so flat that we could see outside and could not resist the urge.

'Quick,' Dave said, 'let's not stop here. Let's go for it!'

With that, we began paddling furiously. Then, as we crossed what should be the impact zone or area where most of the waves should be breaking, the first sets began to loom. They were like ghosts rising from the depths, light green against a pastel grey background peppered with snowflakes. Luckily, we had enough momentum to punch through the first of these waves.

Now sucking ice-cold air, we gasped, heaved and lunged forward. It was difficult to identify where this elusive, safe place beyond the break was. So, to be sure we just kept up the pressure, pumping frantically.

Then Dave exclaimed, 'Think we're okay now!'

We stopped, and turned our boards towards shore. To our amazement, we were so far out that only the top of Knocknarea

Mountain could be seen. Up there, there is a mound which houses the grave of Queen Maeve, but it was white with snow. None of those thoughts seemed to matter at that moment.

It took only seconds and the sea returned to its enormous self. Now the real sets began to arrive. We shuddered at the sight. Dave, full of composure, selected an enormous wall and paddled furiously on its face. He dropped down almost perpendicular, and with a cry of achievement, went shooting away with style and panache. He whooped and whooped and then was gone far inside. Then it dawned that I had not caught anything yet, and was therefore quite alone. When this happened before, it was the tropics, warm and friendly, but here, it was very different. Very different!

Isolated and in a state of increasing hysteria, I turned the board towards shore and paddled as fast as possible in front of the next approaching wall. I felt the wave push me forward, and in a moment of premature triumph dropped down its face. I cut hard right and as I did so things just got darker and darker till with a boom I was submerged in the freezing depths. As I did not have a leash, my board was instantly whisked away. On breaking surface, I just had time for a gasp of air and then the next aquatic freight train rolled over. This ghastly turbulence repeated its thunderous punishment, over and over again, and I became desperate. In those days, I did not wear a helmet and the rubber hood was not very warm – it let in water and with every plunge my forehead was gripped with pain. I tried to breathe, but could hardly manage: that north Atlantic air mixed with excitement was like a lethal cocktail! Then, perhaps it was my cries to the Almighty or my mother's prayers, but the turbulence stopped. I gathered myself and said,

'Look, you are about to become a long-distance swimmer, so get busy.'

I looked hard for my board but it was out of sight. By now I had been pushed back from the impact zone to where the waves peak up but do not really break. This was the zone that had lured us out in the first place. This was unhealthy territory for me as it was almost push-less because it was a deep channel. This meant I had little to propel me in, and worse still, the rip was pushing me to the right. Then a gigantic set arrived and rolled all the way through. This one was so big it helped carry me in about fifty feet, just enough to begin seeing the shore. At best, a wetsuit will keep you afloat. They are okay if you swim on your back, but if you try to swim face-down they are cumbersome. Eventually, between a mixture of backstroke and crawl, and finally a rip-roaring shore break, I arrived exhausted on 'terra firma'.

I was met by a worried gang, who thought I had been lost because they had retrieved my board at the water's edge. Dave smacked me on the back, just to see that I was not a ghost, and explained that when he rode in he pulled out just before the shore break and tried to paddle out to me. However, the waves had got so heavy that he could not make it. Dave added that if things had gone wrong he would have claimed the board as 'abandoned at sea'. Even Lloyds could not dispute that!

Just then several more Tramore lads joined us and quickly got in for a white-water surf. Willie Parks, kindly offered the use of his Bar ballroom for dressing but at the same time opened the bar service hatch. Willie, all smiles was at our service. So the evening developed into a half-on, half-off wetsuit party. I took it all in, and later enjoyed writing about the occasion for our club newsletter 'Surfer Brag'.

Lifeboat Wake Surfing

Soon after that, we got news that Duke Kahanamoku had suffered a fatal heart attack at the Waikiki Yacht Club and died on January 22, 1968. His death marked the passing of a world-class athlete, though sadly, not only did he never surf in Ireland, he never fulfilled his ambition to play golf there either. Soon after that another event in the United States on April 4th, 1968 was to have profound consequences not only there, but also to the hotel business in Ireland. It was the assassination of Martin Luther King Jr. in Memphis, Tennessee. As he was the father of the African American Civil Rights movement, his sacrifice was to stir the souls of many people, notably in the north of Ireland where they felt similar issues needed to be addressed. We surfers were impressed by the developments but did not foresee the consequences.

For us in our little world, it was time for a surf-in with the guys from the north. We chose Sligo for the venue and as usual we the disciples, arrived in bad weather with heavy seas breaking along the Bundoran coast. The only shelter we could find was the gently curved beach of Mullaghmore. There were the usual people present – Harry, Roger, Dave Kenny, Hughie O'Brien-Moran and a few others. From Donegal and the north there were Ted Alexander, Bo Vance, Martin Lloyd, Charley Adjey and some more of their crew. The combined group surfed some chest-high waves that crashed without shape. But we had a good time socialising and comparing notes. Then we went to Bundoran where large waves were breaking on the point, now known as the peak. I met several of the canoeists, headed by Derek Martin and Ernest Lawrence. They entered the sea at the quay on the south side of Bundoran while we proceeded to paddle across the flat water and out to the middle of the bay. I left my camera with someone and as a result got recorded riding the soup that day. However, as expected I lost my board and spotted it floating right beside the point. When I eventually got there, I was relieved to find the rocks were covered in a growth that made them soft to touch. This meant that neither the board nor I got dinged.

Back in Bray, I joined the newly formed Bray Junior Chamber of Commerce and the committee said they would attempt to hold Bray's first ever sea festival. They laid on an air show and they also said the Dun Laoghaire lifeboat would be coming to demonstrate water safety. I therefore phoned the coxswain in advance, and asked it they would tow me onto their wake and take a film of the event. He agreed and I therefore brought the lifeboat coxswain our 8mm movie camera and a thick rope in advance. The day of the sea festival was bright and sunny, and the beach was crowded. When the lifeboat arrived, I gingerly paddled out, and they passed me the rope after tying it to the stern. Then with a roar I was towed in a standing position behind the lifeboat. The speed was kept to a minimum because that would create the highest wake possible which reached near chest high. I pulled myself hand over hand close to the wake till to my delight I tipped over the front of the foam and began to surf freely along. This was real tow-in surfing. Though I came off the wave a few times, they stopped and set me going again and again till I had completed two lengths of Bray beach. For me it was fun, for them it was kindness, and unfortunately for the onlookers it meant very little! The film is included in the 7th section of youtube DVD called 'Dawn'.

Beach Access

Beach access had never been a problem but the issue would eventually arise in Doonbeg, Co. Clare, where solicitors working on behalf of the West Coast Surf Club managed to secure access to the beach through a golf course. Problems began to arise when farmers or landowners, took exception to people crossing their land to get to a surf break. In the east, this sort of problem was off to an earlier start. The north of the city had an abundance of sandy beaches open to the public but to the south the first sandy beaches lay at least twenty-five kilometres away and that is where the problem begins. To explain, heading south, the first beach with problem is Magheramore. It lies a half a mile south of Blain Row golf club, at the end of a very long laneway, down which we used to drive. In 1968 a new owner, Mr Cooney, locked the gate. Our club began to negotiate with Mr Cooney who agreed to leave the key of the entrance gate in a farmhouse for our use, provided we took out insurance to cover our members against accident. This plan cost us IR£12, worked well for one winter, until one day he opened the gate permanently. Recently the problem began again because a new owner so everyone must once again park on a busy road and walk.

The next gem was Magherabeg, which when translated means small – yet this beach is larger than Magheramore! This is a conservation area but the public have no access and it is therefore more or less inaccessible and hence forgotten. Next to this beach lie's Jack's Hole and McDaniel's caravan park, with access to the cliff beaches and the north end of Brittas Bay. Jack's Hole has a promontory protecting it on the south side, and a curve of sand dunes backed by shallow cliffs. This provided the dawn surfers with some varied breaks until it also was closed. People were always prepared to pay at the gates for entry to both areas. However, both of these sections, Jack's Hole and the caravan park, were bought by new owners who only permitted their mobile home owners entry. The new owner of Jack's Hole bulldozed the sand dunes flat in the 90's and inserted mobile homes where the public once enjoyed leisure. These two actions effectively blocked off access to five beaches, all of which had a wave of some shape or other and were vital 'keep fit' areas for the people of south county Dublin and surrounding areas.

Moving a little further south, we find that Wicklow Council opened two large car parks at the centre and south end of Brittas Bay beach, but then proceeded demolished a huge dune on the south end and close the barriers from September to mid-June. This effectively blocks off winter sea sports almost all together. However, at the extreme south end of the beach there is a small all-year parking strip that will take about a dozen cars. That is the only parking that exists during nine and half months of the year. Finally, just next to this and in an elevated position, there was a landowner who permitted parking on his adjoining field. There were stairs down to a large sheltered beach close to the long promontory at the south end of the bay called Mizzen Head. This beach was very popular with families in the summer, but now lies empty due to lack of access – one more beach lost. 1

1. Many years later we put this whole case in writing to Wicklow Co. Council and directly to Martin Cullen TD, who had the responsibility (Ref 3759/mc/03). In the end, there was little done by the council to improve the situation.

Down South

In June of 1968, the club decided to take an exploratory trip to Inchydoney and send word out about the intended venue. This small resort comprises of two beaches with a tiny headland in the middle and a river at each end. The river on the left side of the bay is quite powerful and causes a well-shaped wave to form as the swell meets the outflow. We had our first experience of good waves at this location. This was also a family outing. Vivienne, who is Harry's daughter, was using a new board that Roger had made for her. She was quite excited and so we watched her catch countless waves in brilliant sunshine. This was also the occasion when we met up with the Limerick surfers. These were the guys who would very soon take on the role of contest organisers. These were the Sam McCrums, Mike Murphys, Hugh Milns and Pip Cullens of the west, along with their girlfriends.

That evening in the original old world Inchydoney Hotel we gathered in the bar. There was a new member from Clonakilty called Big Sean O'Connell, because of his height. Sean bought specially ordered board eleven feet long from C&S. Now quite worn out from riding his new board, and after a few drinks, Sean pushed forward to give his views, saying,

'Why don't you fellows put sails on the boards? It would make things a lot easier.'

There was a moment of silence, broken only by an outcry from insulted sea gods crying, 'No way, Sean, you're crazy!'

From then on Vivienne, who was Ireland's very first surfer girl, was also accepted as one of the gang. She used to come frequently on trips to the west coast but I often took her along locally when Harry was busy. She recalls:

'He smoked his corn cob while we drove, and never stopped describing waves, it was fun! We just surfed the local spots close by – Killiney, Magheramore or Courtown. Then when I was with Dad and the others, I surprised them with my improved ability in good-sized waves. I knew there were a few other girl members but I wondered if there were other girls out there who were equally competitive as myself.' The answer was soon to be forthcoming;

Wahines

We saw earlier that the Hawaiian islanders were the first stand-up surfers in the world, yet women equally participated and were heroes of the sport. Early engravings from the islands depict half-dressed women perched on surfboards at the top of curling waves. These 'wahines', as they were called, were so respected that one of Oahu's famous breaks, Kekaiomamala, is named after a woman. They had a custom that was most hospitable; it allowed any male and female who ride the same wave the right to marry. This could never happen in Ireland since so many have by now succumbed to the greedy assertion of 'my wave'. Irish surfing legends are still only in the making and it remains a mystery whether an unknown woman in Kerry really surfed Ballyheigue – or was it a myth?

However, there were many girls who began their legend hood, braved the elements, and were as alive as ducks in a pond. In the early Sixties Emcee Britton in Rossnowlagh was a bodyboarder who turned to use one of the Britton family's long boards. She was hooked and became dedicated to the sport. Lifeguards Una Henderson and Patricia Cassidy learned to surf by the same means. To begin it was just fun, and later serious work. In those days, there were no official surf instructors and these girls had to devise the best ways they could to affect a rescue. They quite naturally read all they could about UK and Australian methods.

On the personal front, I had my own stake in the female side of surfing. In 1968 a bunch of hotel management students from the Dublin Hotel School in Cathal Brugha Street visited our hotel as part of their training experience. I had the task of showing them around and giving them a spiel about the business. On this particular occasion, I spotted the cutest female student I had ever seen. She was medium height, very thin, with light fair hair and blue eyes. She was very interested in everything I had to say, which made me feel important. In fact, the group of girls were all very attractive and as it turned out, they were all good friends. There were also some guys but they did not make me feel as elevated, because they asked lots of difficult questions – they called my bluff! When they departed the word of the South Pacific song came into mind:

'Once you have found her never let her go!'

Her name was Ann Kelly, and on our very first date that April when I turned on to her street, I was greeted by rows of fully blooming pink cherry trees. The date was already off to a good start. This was enhanced by a feeling of tranquillity, trust and affection, not only from her, but also from her family; all this added to the love that was brewing in my soul.

I began taking her on surf trips, she tried surfing but preferred just to swim. I introduced her to one and all, and she took an interest in surfing photos. Unknown to her, by doing this she became Ireland's first female surf photographer. Because of her friendly disposition, she made friends with many of the female side of the surfing world. There was Dave Kenny's girlfriend Gill Arnold, who later was to become Dave's wife. Then there was Helen, the wife of Ken Mc, a very early Irish surfer returned from San Francisco. They sported a mustard-coloured VW Beetle that they imported. There was Harry Evans's wife Carmel and daughter Vivienne, who has already been mentioned. There was also the already mentioned Jane Cross from Cork who later formed the Fastnet Surf Club with Tom Flynn; she became a competitive swimmer and represented Ireland abroad. Jane and Vivienne were both picked to represent Ireland on the Irish surf team in the Europeans at Lahinch – an event that sadly never happened. There was also Helena Condon, who studied in Dublin and surfed in Magheramore until she could get home to her native Sligo. Jane Parks from Strandhill, a relation of Willie Parks, was also one of the surfing tribe. Over in Lahinch, there was Henrietta Glendon, who surfed a little to keep in step with Michael Murphy, her lanky fun-loving boyfriend. Some girls with an eye on the future were becoming involved and would soon take the plunge. Linda Byrne, who would motivate many other women to surf, used a board that was specially built for her by her husband Gerard. She also encouraged her sister-in-law Christine to join in.

Now the story is about to slip a bit beyond the 1973 but there has to be exceptions. The first was while all this maritime razzmatazz was going on young girl was sizing up the scene and wondering if they would ever get involved.

This was Hugh O'Brien-Moran's future wife Margaret, who would become a surfer with a difference. Margaret's surfing ability would grow in style and proficiency till eventually she would get fifth place in the European Championship in Scotland, 1981, and represent Ireland in the World event in Puerto Rico. Margaret was also a tough negotiator, and challenged the Irish Surfing Association about why the women's Irish National trophy was inferior by comparison to others - resulting in a new trophy being provided. The second is Barry and Emcee Briton's daughter, Easkey, known as a world class female surfer, who has tackled Tai phoo in Tahiti and even *"Aill Na Searrach"* at the Cliffs of Moher. The third exception was Zoe Lally who was kind enough to share some of her personal experiences to date:

'I started surfing in 1986. My first realisation of surfing in Rossnowlagh was Eurosurf '85. I remember seeing all the countries' flags from my home on the cliffs in Rossnowlagh but had no idea what was going on so I walked across the beach to see what was happening and it was the opening ceremony for Eurosurf. The following summer a letter was pinned to the notice board at my school from the Irish Surfing Association inviting students to come and try surfing at various locations around the coast that summer. Obviously Rossnowlagh was one of the spots and I was there for the first session in June 1986. I was fifteen years old. Roci Allan pushed me into my first wave and I was immediately hooked.'

'I surfed non-stop for the rest of that summer (without a wetsuit). I was back at school when my first wetsuit arrived so I had to wait until the weekend to use it. I hit the beach at dawn that Saturday morning with my brother, John, and we surfed until dark. We were so warm in our new wetsuits we didn't get out of the water all day, resulting in the two of us being really sick that night from dehydration, and we couldn't surf again until the following weekend.'

'Roci was our mentor. He tolerated all our nonsense surf questions, drove us to Bundoran to surf and all over the country to contests. C&S in Bray had been closed a long time, so there were no surf shops in Ireland at that stage, so Roci organised our supply of wax, leashes, boots, gloves, etc. I got my first surfboard from Conor Britton and for years the Smugglers Creek restaurant sponsored me as a competitive surfer. Surfing took me to university in Swansea, Wales in 1989 (I got a sports scholarship which enabled me to continue surfing while studying). Andrew Hill was in his final year in Swansea when I arrived – he looked after me, picked me up at the train station, showed me around and took me surfing when I was supposed to be at my first lecture! In 1992, when I finished university, I moved to Easkey with Tania Ward [woman bodyboarder from Portrush]. I intended staying for a year but nearly twenty years on I am still here. I have made so many friends through surfing, have had so many adventures and have so many stories to tell. I hope to be surfing for a long time to come.'

Also in Tramore there is another dedicated early morning surfer, and that is a girl called Brigitte, who is Henry Moor's wife. Finally, there were two relatives, one being Grace O'Sullivan who was not only a Tramore surfer but winner of the 1981 Women's National Championships. Grace became a local hero as she was one of the protestors on board the Greenpeace Rainbow Warrior at the time it was sunk. The second is her sister Lola who was to become Lord Mayoress of Waterford and who also surfs along with her husband Ronan Breen, one of the founders of the local – T Bay Surf Club.

Legends Galore

Though it was still 1968, the sport was now showing signs of growth. In Bray, though far from the real potential surfing zones of the west, things were far from dormant. Bill Byrne from the Vevay joined the Surf Club of Ireland, and came to see me. He had begun to construct his first board from fibreglass because he wanted to take his two sons, both Gerard and Declan to surf. They were in their teens and very enthusiastic.

Bill invited me to come to his house to see his progress with the board building. I visited, and there in the living room was a well-shaped blank with stringer and fin all quite ready to be glassed. Their mother just loved seeing the boys committed to surfing and had no trouble embracing the sport. In no time, he had the board ready to launch and took it to Magheramore to begin their life's journey of ocean pursuits. They were very inventive and took a different approach from others as they began to blow their own foam, to minimise cost. This permitted them to speedily produce boards while moving forward in style and design. When the boys got older they got girlfriends, Linda and Christine, who both loved to dive but also surf!

It was now a certainty that if one went to Magheramore on any windy day, the two boys would be there grabbing whatever waves they could. There was another person who appeared on the scene

113

while sporting an enormous fat homemade board of his own. Paddy Connick had discussed board-making with the Byrnes, but reckoned that bigger was better. Later, he made another that was more up-to-date and became the first person they knew of who owned a compact motorhome, with wife inside and boards on top. Word also had it that Gareth Hayes and Barry Drinan, made a balsa wood surfboard in Kilkee, and that this craftwork definitely qualified them to attempt at building fibreglass boards. However, it was recognised that at the time no one had yet come up to the standard of Bo Vance the Byrns fibreglass boards

Maheraghmore, was the very same beach that David Deering, who became a very courageous surfer, taught his son Eoin McCarthy Deering the basics of the sport. In years to come and with great effort Eoin managed to become part of the Irish surfing squad, having spent one-year training in Sligo.

Meanwhile, in Rhode Island, USA, Joe McGovern found himself in much the same predicament as we surf lovers in Ireland did: he too had to fight his corner to establish the sport locally. Dealing with this probably came naturally to him, because he was second-generation Irish. Joe lived on the tiny 1,045 square mile state of Rhode Island, which had joined the union in 1790. His state had a small population, nice beaches and fabulous Atlantic waves. Oddly these waves were the ones that travelled the opposite way from those arriving in Ireland, though he had the added advantage of picking up hurricane waves moving up from the south. Joe often read of far-off sunny California, which was just as difficult for him to get to as it was for us in Europe or even Ireland. Five years earlier, in 1963, two Rhode Island surf lifeguards, Matt Chrostowski and Chuck Fogarty, returned from a trip to California with the first surfboards he had ever seen. The circumstances and time frame is not much different than in Ireland. The first surf shops in Rhode Island opened in 1964. That May, Joe's and his brother Don rented boards from the new local Hobie Shop in Narragansett and later bought their first boards that summer. Don picked out a red 9'0" Malibu Custom and Joe got a clear 9'3" Hobie with a ¾" redwood stringer. Learning to surf for them and everyone else was by trial and error. Their only source of wetsuits were the local dive shops who sold the two-piece ¼"-thick dive suits: neoprene legs with a 'beavertail' top which was not designed for paddling and causing abrasive armpits as the suits deteriorated with even modest use – resulting in wetsuit rashes of epic proportions. They also quickly learned that dishwashing gloves were useless in the New England winter, as water temperatures were only a few degrees above freezing. As they became more involved with surfing they wondered about their swell generating storms travelling across the Atlantic, and their effect on 'the other side'. Yet it would over thirty years before Joe chased a swell from Rhode Island to wave prone Ireland.

Around that time another young adventurer was shaping his aquatic future. This was Gerry Collins, who was not planning on becoming a surfer, but would become a canoeist with a difference. Gerry, who lived in Dublin, had decided to move from rivers to riding waves where possible. To do this, he began to travel with his friends to the south end of Brittas Bay where good canoe waves could be found. One day he saw surfers turning into a lane between Wicklow Town and Brittas Bay. So he followed and discovered Magheramore beach. He felt that these surfer waves were more challenging than Brittas Bay or even the rivers he had tried. From that day on, he frequented Magheramore's point break amidst the local surfers – Roger Steadman, Johnny Lee and a few others. In those days that was considered to be a crowd. Gerry had to content himself with using a river canoe in the waves as the shorter, wider surf canoe had not yet been developed. But needless to say, all this experience helped improve his standard. He remained a surf canoeist from then on even though he already knew how to surf on a board. Gerry is admired for doing what he did best, but also, he and his pals were considered to be a good safety factor for wiped-out board riders, as leashes were only beginning to come into fashion. When the wind hit storm force and the waves swung around the point it was consoling to have a kayak nearby. Gerry and his friends soon looked to greener pastures and went south, where they linked up with the Tramore surfers and together they shared trips. Not only that, but they formed a walking club, called the Gowers, and shared hikes on the Comeragh Mountains.

However, some people are legends for odd reasons: In 2011, Ciaran Downes a great surfer from Bray, and I met a man who must have been one step ahead of us all. He was called Gerry Donagher, and he told us that he dragged a tree trunk down the beach at Trá Buí. He and a friend pushed it out into the sea and attempted to ride it to shore. Perhaps in doing that they became the world's first surfing lumberjacks. With that under his belt, now Gerry can spend many happy hours over a pint in Tig Mic Gabaine in his native Easkey, telling his story to one and all.

Lahinch

On the 26 May 1968, the club arranged a surfari to Lahinch. This is the most exciting town in Ireland, I thought. It overlooks an enormous bay, with cliffs to the left and a broad stretch of sand to the right. The beach sweeps for more than a mile to meet a river outlet and a harbour, near the village of Liscannor. This town is now famous for seafood and a memorial to John P. Holland, the inventor of the submarine, but in 1968 none of this had developed. To the left, though they had not yet discovered it, there were some great tubular waves that always broke around a flat rocky curve. This later would later be christened Cornish Point, because the visitors from Cornwall were among the first to use it. Directly in front of the town there were several breaks rolling in different directions – all the way up to high tide, when they hit the promenade for an hour or so, before receding.

We knew about a few guys who went to school in Ennis and had been in touch, but now were becoming interested in forming their own club. The leader of the pack was called Sam McCrum, and he was the only one with a board. Sam persuaded the group, along with Mike Murphy from Limerick, to come to Achill Island, Co. Mayo to surf. Mike asked Sam, 'What's surf?' And very soon he found out. Not only did they surf in Achill, but when they brought their guitar into the pub late at night they only had to strum a few cords and the whole bar erupted in song. As a reward, the owners made sure they had plenty of pints and even a tray of sandwiches to round off the night. There was an American fellow, Mike said, who spent the summer surfing in Achill and did not have enough cash to get to Heathrow for his pre-booked flight to LA, so to alleviate the difficulty, Mike bought his Weber board and sent him on his way. These were the guys who would soon figure out the best way to run a surf club of their own, but they were not around on our weekend.

There were a dozen people on our trip, and we were in top form. Maybe fo me it was because Ann was with me, though her Dad had given her money to pay for her own room – he would have her be an independent lassie! We booked into the Claremont Hotel and joined the gathering in the bar. There was the usual gang, but there was the addition of the fellow with the Citroen car, Noel Haughey and a chirpy Dorothy G. Next morning Bo Vance met us and said that he and Martin Lloyd had tried to get into the bar where we were, but as it was after hours they were not permitted. What a bummer! Bo and Martin moved further up the coast, as they had spotted Crab Island at Doolin on their map, and wanted to investigate. We were a bit less adventurous, and as the waves were very nice, head high, and there was only a light wind at the time, we remained in Lahinch.

It was clear and sunny, and so I gave Ann the Pentax camera and tripod to take pictures. Just three of us got in that day. I put on a short O'Neill wetsuit, mainly to look cool, especially as it was May 27th, my birthday! I noted that the tide was about three hours from high – just right. I selected the red Sumpter stringerless board, and paddled out into head high faces. As the waves looked so friendly, it was almost an effortless exercise, so we just turned and began to take every wave that came our way. Rod's very light board responded magnificently to my efforts. I soon lined up opposite O'Looneys Pub just as a large set appeared. It came in lines of dark blue with turquoise tops wobbling as they travelled inwards. The board sprung forward and dropped down the face of the third wave. I cut right and zipped across its face just ahead of the break. Meantime, Ann faithfully did as bid, and took a photo at the critical moment. In the meantime some of the group, got cold from the increasing sea breeze and retired to sunbathe in an empty swimming pool in the aquatic centre.

On the next trip, it was summer and Roger and Tony Gleeson were there with their families. * After some gentle shoulder-high surfing we gathered in Kenny's Bar once again. One of the boys said, 'Tony, I hear you wrote a poem, let's hear it!'

Tony said quite shyly that it was called 'The Spanish Dancer'. He recited for us, the first two verses of six that he had composed:

> The evening was a bright glow and the salt sea
> smells merging with the Off shore breeze became
> pollen heavy, blossom scented.
> On the reef, the waves were smooth faced.
> Breaking, they meshed with Armada memories
> Of crashing timbers and thin gaunt strangers
> Staggering to the wind-swept shore.
> In the pub the surfers sat, silent now nursing pints,
> remembering the Heaving waves. Waves born in
> distant storms Quickening on the Spanish reef as
> the surfers Dropped, falling and turning, blown by
> The crashing wave wind and racing from the rocks
> below.

In later years both Tony and his wife Maureen, and Roger with his wife Halima, moved to live in Kenya.

Tiger Tim

About two weeks after the May surfari, I got a call from a fellow with a strong west-country English accent:

'This is Tim Heyland, I'm on business in Belfast and I want to come down and see what all this surfing in Ireland is all about.'

'Tim, you realise the real surf is in the west,' I confessed.

'That's okay. I don't have time to go there on this trip but I'll still come down to you.'

After some exchange of details, he rang off.

Wow, I thought, this guy is a tiger, really determined. Later Tim arrived at my Dad's hotel wearing a business suit. He was a thin, wiry guy with fair hair. He brought me up to date on his surfing history. It seems that he had seen a poster for Australia with a surfer perched on a wave. That was in or around 1960. So when his family moved to Brazil he knew just what he would do. Once there, he made a wooden board that he cut to shape with a machete. Soon after that he and a friend began importing boards from California. This was to get him started in business and fund his trip to Hawaii. Tim intended opening a surfboard business in Britain. As it turned out he succeeded in the quest.

I had already got that day off and, by coincidence; there was a massive summer storm raging. The night before the wind had reached Force 9 to 11 southerly, and as well as waves it had left a trail of destruction in its path. Trees were down, roof tiles were off and caravans were turned over. As wind was still raging it meant one thing – Tim was going to see east coast surf.

We strapped the two glass boards on the car. None of the club came with us as they were unable to get time off at such short notice. So, we left Bray about 8.30 a.m. and went to Jack's Hole, just north of Brittas Bay. This place has a long outcrop of rocks and a cliff on its southern side, around which the swell lined up. The surf was enormous and peeling off on a sandbar at the extremity of the headland. The peaks heaved and crashed and then rolled all the way to shore, almost a quarter mile away. I have never seen it like that before or since.

Tim and I paddled out in the shelter of the rocks and when ready just drifted into the line-up. We did not need wetsuits, as the wind was very warm and we liked the freedom. Almost immediately we both caught waves and rode them all the way to shore. Tim had a powerful bear-like stroke that would make any board take off. I was much more laid back and lacked Tim's determination.

After a time there, we pulled on T-shirts and drove in wet board shorts for two hours till we got to Tramore. I phoned Dave Kenny and told him we were on the way. This time we would look at the hurricane at Tramore Strand – face on. Surfing there was out of the question, though Tim went out just for the fun. Dave advised we should go to Kilmurren – or Ballysmell, as he called it. This is a unique keyhole-shaped bay that is at its best when the conditions are chaotic. The waves crash and break in the mouth of the inlet, which is only about 150 yards wide. Then they re-form and spill into the saucer-shaped interior. This makes them very thick and slow to break but make for some really fun surfing. Several other lifeguards arrived with their new boards procured from us at C&S Surfboards. These guys were already good surfers and this was their patch. They had learned fast from lots of practice and from being fit and sea-wise. Tim was impressed with the turnout, and a great hurricane day was had by all. By now lots of people were asking for boards and with C&S in operation word spread. It was time to order more stock to show and sell, but also to get in a few boards on trial from Tim's Company.

Trouble Ahead

A general meeting of the Surf club of Ireland, was held in the North Star Hotel in Dublin to facilitate the guys and girls that would have to travel from the country. By now the club had seventy members and there were all sorts of questions being asked by those who lived far away. I opened the meeting but was apprehensive, and as it turned out this was justified.

To begin with, I felt quite out of my depth in this new environment, as there were some strange faces in the crowd. The problem was that some people had developed their own agendas, and begun to voice disapproval with the way things were being done. A breakup was imminent. Roger stepped in and fielded the most questions. Being a skilled businessman, he was capable of parry and thrust in the face of unsavoury questions. He did fine for a while but eventually a clanger was dropped.

'Chairman,' said one of the boys from somewhere north or north-west. 'We want to know more about club finances – where did you get all this money to do all the publicity trips, contests and other surfing things you do?'

Roger, Harry and I were stumped, as we had not expected to be landed in a financial question time. Also, the club had almost no funds because almost no one bothered to pay the fee. Harry responded,

'We paid for the National contest with Pepsi Cola sponsorship. Then we supplemented it all with our own money. There are no beneficiaries, we just took the loss and did it for surfing.'

By now the meeting was upset. People were into something deeper than they expected. They felt uncomfortable and because of the doubts cast, they too began to ask as many difficult questions as could be asked. Now we were the bad guys and would have to demonstrate our dedication in a different way than before.

One of the questions asked was, 'Does the club have a constitution?'

Roger, Johnny, Harry and I looked at one another.

Harry took the question and in crisp military manner replied, 'No, there has not yet been a need.'

'Well if we are going to be members of this club,' they responded, 'we want a constitution so we know what people are up to!'

This rather basic request hit the committee like a second bolt out of the blue. It was the timing and the context in which it was presented and the underlying accusation that hurt. So instead of talking surf, from then on we spent many meetings and phone calls arguing about legislation. Eventually we managed to hammer out a constitution. Nevertheless, nature took its course and the guys from the north told us they were forming their own club. This was the end of the Pollyanna days of Irish surfing and the beginning of adulthood. Also, it prompted more groups to break away and form other clubs. This meant that there would now be an urgent need for an Irish Surfing Association to bind us all together

Very soon, it was time for another meeting so as to sort out the constitution and other issues. We tied in the meeting with a surfari to Strandhill. We concluded the trip with the meeting, which took place in the Silver Swan Hotel, Sligo. It began in a very subdued atmosphere, with our club now hoping to ratify a constitution so there would be no more obstacles. This was accepted, and the northern boys informed us that their new name would be the North Shore Surf Club.

As I chaired the meeting, I notice an unusual on the list that said 'Tramore issue'.

At that point Dave 'Dukie' Kenny responded to the entry and stood up to speak. He ran his fingers through his mop of blond hair, and with a face bronzed from the sun, he turned to the crowd and said:

'Fellows, we have just formed a new club, our own club in Tramore.'

There was a gasp and Ann and Vivienne began to shed a tear, as they had figured, in their innocence that we were all a sort of family that would never split up. In a sense, they were not wrong about that assumption because we were also constructing our Association.

Dave Kenny went on to say, 'It will be called the South Coast Surf Club.'

Eamon 'Camel' Matthews and Hugh O'Brien-Moran both nodded in confirmation of what Dave had said. After the meeting, the consensus was that it was not a bad idea, and it meant that surfing was expanding in its own natural way. Now, it became easier to say, 'Congratulations to all at the new South Coast Surf Club.'

Soon after that Tom Flynn and Jane Cross wrote to say that they had started the Fastnet Surf Club in Cork, and right after that Eddie Comer of Lahinch announced that they had already formed the new West Coast Surf Club. Now it was paramount that an Association was quickly ratified, as Brian told us the Rossnowlagh Surf Club was now up and running and open to membership.

CHAPTER 11

Surfari to France

At the other end of the spectrum things were developing in a European direction. We were hoping to go to France but here were mass riots on the streets of Paris, and two thirds of the French workforce was on strike. This had begun in March 1968 and though it is now June there had been no let up. Therefore, Colm and I planned to meet Roger and Rosemary in Jersey, Channel Islands so as to wait out developments. Roger Steadman confirmed that he and Rosemary would come by hydrofoil from Guernsey, where they were visiting Rosemary's parents. While waiting for them, Colm and I drove to St Ouen's Bay, which is a long straight two-mile-long beach. The waves heavy and overhead and it took a long time to struggle outside, and get used to the size. Eventually after many attempts a few friendly waves arrived and I surfed them with success. By taking these few rides, I now felt part of the scene. We laughed when we discovered that the local lifeguards had caught a dozen crabs, filled a barrel with seawater and built a fire to boil the water and cook their bounty. They then pigged out and collapsed to sleep it off in the sun.

Next day Roger and Rosemary arrived as planned. Rosemary was looking magnificent with her Guernsey tan and floral dress. Roger said with excitement and a confident chuckle,

'Lads, I gather from the latest news that the student riots are under control so we should be okay to go to Biarritz.'

We hastily booked on the hydrofoil and went to Le Havre, where we picked up a rented car with a roof rack suitable for two boards. The first was Roger's prized white ten-foot Bilbo that he had brought to Ireland originally, the other was my new yellow nose-rider. Rosemary had other ideas, because she had a Michelin good food guidebook, and also insisted that we make our first stop at a delicatessen to buy *dejeuner*. A half hour later, found us lying beside *le voiture*, drinking wine and devouring French bread spread with pâté and Camembert. We even drifted asleep in the heat of the sun. Typical of the times, there was no interference from the gendarmerie and we needed the rest. God be with those days, they were full of innocence!

When, the next day, we eventually drove into sun-drenched Biarritz, we began to have the time of our lives. We went mainly to the Côte des Basques beach on the south side, and rode shoulder-to head-high waves. In those days, even France did not have too many surfers so we had quite a bit of room to ourselves. On the first day, we lunched by the edge of the sea on the concrete steps, where Rosemary's pâté and cheese revived us. We had bought cheap red wine, but it stained our lips purple. From there on we upped the budget for better quality plonk.

We also went to Guéthary, a point break further down the coast towards Spain. It is overlooked by high palisades of plants and trees and seats – very picturesque. The swell was still head-high and when it hit the point it seemed to bend around and move to the right. Roger and I had a great session sharing waves and enjoying the freedom of not having to wear wetsuits.

When we came back to shore, a voice shouted, 'Hello, Roger and Kevin!'

It was David Sumpter, Rodney's brother.

'How are you and how's Rodney these days?' I asked.

David frowned and said, 'Sorry to say it, but Rod has had a serious knee injury and cannot surf now.'

Next day we went to Hendaye, (1) but the swell was not getting in, so we returned to Biarritz and tried our skills at Grande Plage. This shelving beach is for more serious surfing and breaks left and right but always close to shore.

A week later we sadly headed north to get the ferry home. As Roger drove through a tiny French hamlet, a gendarme stopped the car. He did not speak English but looked aggressive and began to poke at the baggage. Then he indicated that he wanted the cases opened.

Roger was taken aback and said, 'Look, this is ridiculous.'

With that the cop demanded all passports, turned and, with our precious documents, walked back towards the hamlet. I decided that I was not going to let our passports out of sight and followed the gendarme: Where e'er the passport go-eth, there go I. I thought!The gendarme strutted about 200 yards and turned into a tiny house which was the police station. I stumbled in behind him and came face to face with an officer who was behind a desk.

'Pardon, monsieur. Do you speak English?'

He looked blankly at me and mumbled, 'Oui – yes, a little.'

'Sir, why are we being held?'

'Because your friend said ze officer was a pig.'

I recalled Roger's words: 'This is ridiculous.' Then in a flash I realised something.

'My friend said, ridiculous – 'culous' – you might have thought he said 'cule'!' The gendarme's eyes opened and his face relaxed. Just then Roger arrived and erupted into a major defence, saying that he had called no one a pig. By then the centime had dropped and they understood the misconception. With that, the atmosphere changed and they immediately gave back the passports and told us to scram. It was the most welcome scram we ever had!

Roger Steadman in Cote de Basque, France

When we returned from France, I took Ann to dinner and told her all about the trip. That evening I could not contain myself and asked her to marry me. She was quite taken aback, but gathered her composure and replied, 'I'll let you know.'

Now it was my turn to be taken aback, so I giggled nervously and at the same time I agreed to wait. About three weeks later, while we were enjoying a dinner, she said, 'The answer to your question is yes.' But in the heat of the moment, I had forgotten what the question was. Oops!

1. Overlooking Hendaye there is Château d'Abbadie, which was built by an Italian fellow whose parents reared him in Ireland. He lived in Merrion Square during the late 1800s.

He later moved to France where he married a local girl from Hendaye. In the chateau, he has shamrock and Islamic wall designs, an observatory, and he was awarded the Légion d'honneur for his work charting the movement of celestial bodies.

Second National Contest

In September 1968, the Surf Club of Ireland once again ran a national and international contest in Tramore. We were still the voice of surfing in Ireland, though that was in decline. This contest followed the same format as before, and it was another near-success.

Paul Kenny and Eamon Matthews in Annestown Co Waterford

That is to say, that though we were again sponsored by Pepsi Cola, there were delays in getting the event started. The reason was the late arrival of the caravan for judging. We had arranged well in advance that the Caravan for judging should be in place the evening before, but it was not there as promised. We called to talk with the person responsible told him that the caravan was not yet in position, and that it would cause difficulties if delayed till tomorrow – the contest day. He was a bit offhand but insisted it would be on the prom first thing the following morning, along with the PA system

Unfortunately, it did not arrive until about 10.30 a.m., and thus, it was another hour before the show got under way. Just before the caravan's arrival, I was blazing up the town in my Vauxhall to collect some gadgetry and intending to get back in time for the start of contest but crashed into another car. This was sorted out quickly because I admitted full liability.

Meantime, down at the beach, the heat's got under way and at the same time a very special person was being inaugurated into the sport. This was Tom O'Brien from Cork. Tom wrote later:

'When I was in a school for the deaf children in Dublin at the age of fourteen, I came across a picture of someone surfing a huge wave, and was instantly intrigued. As I read I became more and more interested in waves and their wonders. As I turned twenty-two and returned to work after the summer holidays, I was chatting with one of my co-workers and he told me about Tramore. Hence, the following weekend me and my friend Bernard Hegarty headed there to check out this surfing malarkey. One look at the sport in action and I was hypnotised. Therefore, from the 1968 Tramore contest onwards, I became a dedicated surfer.'

True to his promise, Rodney Sumpter had returned as a competitor and brought with him a bunch of Cornish and Welsh surfers to take part in the event. Rod once again took first place in the International section. In triumph, he held his winning trophy over the waves of Tramore and kissed the metal. Despite having the luxury of my old yellow Bilbo nose-rider, shaped by Rodney, I failed to get first place, and had to settle for second. The competition standard was rising rapidly. The winner of the National event was Ted Alexander from Co. Down, who hung on doggedly to every wave he rode and just could not be dislodged.

The seafront became jammed with people and there was a great atmosphere. Ann accompanied me this time and said how she loved the Tramore people. She had a soft spot for Hugh O'Brien-Moran, his brothers Greg and Niall and of course their dad, 'the

'Doc'. There was also a very unique feature – the arrival of a beach lifesaving team from Cornwall. They demonstrated how to line up a team of lifeguards with a rope and torpedo-shaped float, then how one should swim through the waves to a drowning person and how to draw them safely back to the beach. It was all regimented with whistle-blowing, and resembled what Pathé News would show of a Bondi Beach rescue. These life-saving professionals added a lot of glamour to the event and illustrated to the public just how much respect one should have for the sea. The following day, just as the year before, several of the visiting pioneers set off to tour the west. After waving them adios it was time to get back into the sea. The surf that morning was very good and the wind was semi-offshore; I spied nice walls breaking over by the pier under the cliffs. Along with Ann, I took my Rod Sumpter nose-rider and paddled out of the harbour mouth – just like I had often done in Greystones. I left the camera with Ann to click a few photos. The sky was clear blue and the air chilly. The sea was sandy cream colour, and there was lots of torn weed floating about. In moments, I was in position to catch a wall or two. The first I caught was a perfectly shaped left, so I obeyed and enjoyed a fast ride that improved my position for the next encounter. I caught a few more rides and also copied Rod by first standing up, then sitting down on my board for show – but I never tried a head stand! Then, just as I was getting out, Dave Kenny, who lived in a house called Pier View perched on the Doneraile walk that loomed above, arrived at the pier breathless.

'Hey, you guys, I looked out my window this morning and saw an apparition. Someone riding great waves! Any left?'

Dave ploughed into the sea like he had just discovered it for the first time and gave a demo of his own surfing before the tide got too high and the waves faded away. We all had a great laugh about Dave sleeping in, when the waves below his house were breaking so nicely. Originally, I had ordered a radical new Bilbo board and it had arrived in time for the contest. It was less than six feet and narrow. In simple terms, I just could not ride it, nor did I have the patience to learn. During the contest, I did a bunch of deals. I sold both the first red Bilbo and my Sumpter stringerless board, but kept the yellow nose-rider. Then, in a panic, I swapped my new six-foot board for a V-bottom, wide-tailed, eight-foot board, with a huge, dangerous dagger fin that had been owned by one of two South African visitors. This meant that I had the option of using a ten-foot or an eight-foot board, and as a result I felt I was making progress.

Before leaving the town, we met the Tramore Tourist Board and complained about the late arrival of the caravan. In hindsight, this was not a good meeting, and maybe we should have let the caravan issue go. In any case it did not matter, because it was obvious from friendly comments that next time around another county should hold the championships – and Lahinch was already the front-runner. Before his departure, Rod told the group about the planned Second World Surfing Contest and asked would Ireland apply. We told him that it was unlikely that we could repeat all that had happened in 1966. Sponsorship of that magnitude would be hard to get and we would probably not attend. Rod told us that the ISF (International Surfing Federation) rules stated that each country chooses its own team, and passports were not checked by the ISF. Rod then asked if he could represent Ireland if he failed to qualify for the UK team. Our SCI committee, who were still the only voice of surfing in the Ireland, reckoned that as he had done so much for the sport in this country we would agree, and said at the same time that he would have to pay his own way, fly an Irish flag that we would give him, and not ride a board with a flag on the deck other than ours. Rod was grateful and promised to abide by the request.

CHAPTER 12

Intercounty Championships 1968

On the way to the first Intercounty competition in Rossnowlagh we went by way of Ballina, then travelled along the coast towards Sligo, and discovered Easkey. The tide was high at the time and the sea was breaking up against the rocky shore. I took one look and condemned the place to the demons of the deep. This, I thought, was way too dangerous for surfing. On arrival at Rossnowlagh we met Brian Britton, who said,

'I hear you went to Easkey! The Cornish lads have just come back from surfing there. They loved it!'

Now another new idea was in the air. Vinnie Britton wrote to the club and said that his family would present the Intercounty Cup, to be run in October each year. By now his family had grown up and were big fellows, deadly interested in surfing. Brian instantly became the organiser of the event, and delegated some of the running to his brothers and to members of his club which was now evolving. Conor being the eldest got the job of managing the bar. Brian reckoned that was the next best job to surfing.

The hotel had already constructed a clubhouse and an area suitable for storing boards, changing, meeting and marking score cards for contests while sheltered from the elements. All this activity demonstrated clearly that Rossnowlagh meant business.

The idea of an Intercounty was much appreciated and generated lots of excitement. Now, for the first time the sport was not just for individuals, but would be a team event. Immediately Sligo, Donegal, Antrim, Down, Clare and Waterford were destined to be neck and neck as the finalist counties. We, the east-enders – Dublin, Wicklow and Kildare – were now likely to play second fiddle, but we didn't mind; we always knew that west was best. We did not have the consistent surf for practice, and therefore had limitations. This, we knew, was going to be a great family surfing event, and truly it has remained that way to this very day.

The event was run on a trial-and-error basis, with errors being at a minimum. People on teams had to get used to being first in their heat yet not qualifying for the next round. This was because the overall team marks could fall short. If one looks at it the other way around, a lesser surfer could luckily be part of a winning team. To crown it all, Vinnie Britton presented an enormous cup, which in that year was won by Co. Down. The cup was presented to Ted Alexander, the county captain, on the beach, while I stood close by braving the September cold without a wetsuit and sporting yellow board shorts from California. * There was a very nice team picture with Harry, Roger and someone unknown holding Pat Kinsella's board. Happily, for us, these pictures were spread across the county's newspapers. The term 'Intercounty' smacks of rural life and thus generated lots of good will, not to mention that it was also very much a local event. The Donegal team on that day was represented by Conor, Brian and Barry Britton, who else! The final results of the first ever Intercounty Surfing Championships (1968) were as follows:

Down 70 points, Waterford 69, Antrim 67.

In the following year, 1969, Waterford came first because they had a very good team who were prepared to go the distance. They came in force, year after year, despite the difficult trek from Waterford to Donegal and back. Then, as luck would have it for some close neighbours, the Antrim team clawed its way back to the top and remained there for a further five years. One reason was their two-star surfers – Alan Duke and Dave Govan. Alan was one of Ireland's most creative surfers, loaded with courage and agility and, what's more, Alan was and still is an artist, whose oils are of a very high standard and usually depict the ocean and surfing. Dave Govan was training to be a schoolteacher and rode his board with deadly precision, while always looking composed. Ted Alexander, Martin Lloyd, Brian Farthing and John Boomer were the people who rotated, depending on their availability. This is how the results looked when listed:

Inter County Contest, winning team, Ted Alexander is presented with the cup by Vinnie Britton on Rosnowlagh strand with the author on the right in the background, October 1968.

1968: Down – Ted Alexander, Dave Govan, Martin Lloyd

1969: Waterford –Hugh O'Brien-Moran, Eamon Matthews, Derek Musgrave

1970: Antrim – Ted Alexander, Dave Govan, John Boomer

1971: Antrim – Dave Govan, Alan Duke, Martin Lloyd

1972: Antrim – Dave Govan, Alan Duke, Ted Alexander

1973: Antrim – Dave Govan, Alan Duke, Brian Farthing

Eamon Matthews throws in a few recollections:

'The Intercounty contests at Rossnowlagh were always something to look forward to with the prospect of the latest surfing flick and a session or two at the Bundoran reef. From '68 Hugh and I were regulars on the team, drafting in various others as necessary to form the group. These were sought-after positions for a while, but scoffed at later.'

Barry Britton added:

'The Intercounty Surfing Contest was set up, as you already know, in 1968 with the idea of having a contest that the best individual surfer wouldn't always win, and let's face it, it turned out to be more of an end-of-season party than contest. Everyone enjoyed the heats on the Saturday but soon learned it was a big mistake to do too well – because with the shenanigans on a Saturday night one would be a mess on Sunday morning. And if your team had made it into the quarterfinals you were under the spotlight. The reason for there being such a party was that it was the end of season and my brother Conor intended to send the beer barrels back empty. Conor ran the Surfers Bar like a rock venue with bands, and only closed the bar on Sunday evening when all the barrels were emptied. Those were the days!'

The Third Nationals

The third National Championships were held in Lahinch in September 1969. This was the opportunity for the newly formed West Coast Surf Club to show their mettle. The committee and driving force behind the event was the now ex school boy, Sam McCrum from Ennis, Hugh Milne, Mike Murphy and Brian Cusack from Limerick all whom we now knew well. Locally there were Des Deeney, M.J. O'Donnell, Gill Cullen, Frank McEnnis and Eddie Comer, whose family owned a hostelry called Comer's Bar. There was also Antoin (Tony) O'Looney, who some years later would own a more strategically placed bar overlooking the bay and who also paddled across the English Channel for charity. There was also Mike Murphy's girlfriend, Henrietta Glendon, who had the drive and the humour to encourage things to happen.

As you would expect, they commandeered the aquatic centre as a judging area for the event. Now they had given Lahinch a new dimension to its tourist potential. Their god's eye view of the event from the ivory office in the sky gave the West Coast Surf Club an admirable status. Just as policy already dictated, experienced members from all clubs were invited to sit up there and do their stint of judging. Mike and Henrietta were very busy checking and rechecking the work, and posting the resulting information on a leaderboard at pedestrian level. Sam McCrum was beach marshal, and some of the female members sold West Coast Surf Club T-shirts. We from the east also helped with the judging.

I knew that this was a header for future events – the centre was perfect and so also was the town and surroundings. If we ever had a European event this could be the venue. On the day the wind was onshore, and this meant, as usual, that while there would be waves galore, unfortunately they would not be of the quality hoped for. As the heats progressed I took my turn at the judging and therefore had a grandstand view of an immensely long ride taken by Brian Cusack. He took off opposite the centre and travelled at high speed across a head-high wave to his right, ending two hundred yards away, close to O'Looney's Bar. For this he was awarded a well-earned ten out of ten – a rare gift from any judges – thus winning the heat.

Now people like Michael Vaughan of Vaughan's Hotel began to take note. Golfing was their main source of business but in an ever-changing world Michael saw potential and threw his weight behind the sport. He was highly influential on the Limerick/Shannon Tourist Board, and put in a good word about the sport. Carmel Evans later recalled that they had a very happy weekend, because the whole family of nine stayed in Mrs Barrett's guesthouse opposite the church in the centre of town. They enjoyed great breakfasts, and those siblings who did not care for the sea always knew just where to find their dad, Harry. All they had to do was step out the door, look right and there he would be, out in ocean along with Roger, Johnny and the probably me.

Mike Murphy – Murf the Surf – later recalled some of the antics of the West Coast Surf Club members:

'Following the National Championships there was a surfari to the south, but would you believe, it was spread out over two weeks because the ultimate target was north. Here is what happened. The first week of the trip was hosted by the South Coast Surf Club and it consisted mainly of six Norfolk surfers and one Welsh. This huge surfari spent most of the week at Slea Head and the Brandon Bay area, where magnificent five- to eight-foot tubes were experienced. Then they turned north, and returned to Lahinch where they found flat conditions. Monday dawned fresh and Sam McCrum, Hugh Milne and a few stragglers left Lahinch and journeyed north, ignoring all till they arrived at the Belmullet peninsula. They discovered a secluded little strand called Cross Point that had some beautiful five-foot lefts. Forward ho! They headed to Enniscrone and then Easkey, where they found very good waves. This reminded

Sam of La Barre in France, but it was high tide and breaking on the rock face, so they gave it a miss.'

'They finally went through Bundoran and ended up in Rossnowlagh as planned, so as to compete in the second Intercounty surfing championships. This event provided the west coast contingent with a very enjoyable weekend. On Saturday morning, we experienced some beautiful surf, which caused many of us retire indoors by midday. To our delight there was a disco that night, but for various reasons many of our members retired early. However, Sammy made up for us with his antics and his prize-winning strip!'

'Next day we learned that the results were in the following order: Waterford, Antrim, Fermanagh, Clare, Limerick. That evening the Britton's as usual provided a great dinner and we all wandered home eventually to Lahinch, where at last we became the proud owners of our first clubhouse. At that time Eddie Stewart came home from Australia and took up residence in Sligo. Eddie did not join any club but, like many, evolved as a loner who enjoyed surfing with close friends or family and could be called one of Ireland's first 'sole surfers'.

While this was happening, a young American boy was driving through the Bundoran area with his parents. It was 1969, and the Naughtons from Huntington Beach had come to revisit relatives in Galway. It's a pity I did not know them when I was there in '66. Kevin Naughton was a teenager and bored to death because he had tasted the surf scene in Huntington and up to now reckoned that this island 'sucked'. Then in Bundoran he saw a large, well-formed wave peeling off the rocky promontory in the centre of the bay. He said it was crying out to be ridden.

He shouted to his parents to stop the car. They didn't because they held that one should keep away from the sea, unless one wanted to get drowned. But he now knew of Ireland's potential and vowed to return as soon as possible and do what good surfers do. Kevin went on to become a world-class surfer, taking on such giants as the forty-foot wave in Maui called Jaws (Pe'ahi). With this under his belt he knew he could handle almost anything the Atlantic could throw at him and his return to Ireland became imminent. It was the mid Seventies when Kevin fulfilled his ambition and returned here – to an Ireland that had taken several body blows but was ready for a metamorphosis or a renaissance which would be partly brought about by the fabulous input from that great Californian who adopted Ireland as his pet hobby.

Team Goes Overseas

With the accumulation of overseas contacts, some of the Irish clubs began to follow the competition trail. Attending another World event was out of the question, but a European event following the Nationals in Lahinch was of interest. We had learned that the 1969 event would be in Jersey, and this was a must. Already in Rossnowlagh Brian had established the rudiments of Surf Instruction for beginners and also RTE's Mike Murphy made a short film of one of our get togethers but he laced it with comedy.

So, to make up our team the clubs rallied as many of the old brigade as possible and this included guys from North Shore, Tramore, Wicklow and Dublin. This crew were Ireland's first overseas team of contestants. This gallant bunch of ambassadors was photographed at Dublin Airport proudly standing with boards aloft, ready to board a plane. The photo included Eamon Matthews, Davie Govan, Harry Evans, Alan Duke, Bo Vance, Dave Kenny and myself. The picture was published in the Irish Press.

The event was sponsored by Players Number 6 cigarettes and hosted by the Jersey Surf Club, run by Reg Prytherch and Steve Harewood. The team got on well with these blokes, who expressed delight at having Ireland enter for the first time. The big names were Gordon Burgis, Bob Male and, again, Steve Harewood of

Jersey, Chris Jones, Roger Mansfield and Charles Williams of England, and also two very well-known fellows, Rodney Sumpter and Tigger Newling. It was there that we met Tim Heyland once again as he vigorously promoted his Tiki surfboards. Now at last we were beginning to encounter the people who made surfing tick on this side of the world.

Some of the guys hired cars, and I once again got a Mini Cooper. We all checked in to the local campsite and quickly went to St Ouen's Bay to limber up. Just as before, the waves were big and challenging, but we loved it. We got to see the list of heats and the times for the following day. There was an invitation for one person to attend the European Surfing Reception in Hotel de France, St Helier. I was elected to go and therefore donned my best blazer and set off. In those days, formal things like that occurred. I met Pam Gough and Doug Wilson of Bilbo. Pam, as it turned out, was the person who processed all orders of boards for us in Ireland; Doug was her manager. These were the mainsprings behind Roger's and my C&S Surfboard agency. It was great to meet them in person and a good business move.

The whole team shared a tent and when I returned the group were giddy and cracking wild jokes. The banter got out of hand, and as there was a camping curfew the attendant arrived with a torch and bellowed for us to shut up or leave. Wow, we thought – how abrupt can one get? The next morning, just for the laugh, we piled all the boards on the tiny car and took some pictures. It was a nice way to get the team together and the shots became something we valued.

Then, as it was the contest day, we headed to St Ouen's Bay. We did our best as usual, but did not qualify. However, at the same time we knew we were gaining valuable experience. When the finals came about, I climbed on the roof of a shed laden with onlookers and took a few photos. As luck had it, I eventually moved away to get a better view – and just in time, as the roof collapsed. A dozen unfortunates fell through the shattered roof and into the hut, getting scraped and quite roughed up. Otherwise the visit was a roaring success.

The winner of the open was event was Gordon Burgis of Jersey, who rode waves that were breaking against the sea wall on high tide. Gordon was used to this backwash effect at high tide as he grabbed each peak as it rose out of nowhere and trashed it before it dissolved. That's the advantage of knowing one's beach. Gordon, from St Helier, was another son of a hotelier. England won the team event and the judging panel included people from South Africa, New Zealand, Australia, France and England, and was headed by Bob Cooper, who was a legend of Californian surfing. However, Bob Cooper was the winner of the individual, giving an amazing demonstration of pure talent on the waves. Ireland at this stage was seen as a sincere and well-behaved (except for the camp site glitch) bunch of nice guys – maybe not winners yet, but with great potential.

Gran Canaria

Taking up where Martin Luther King Jr. left off; on the 1ˢᵗ of January 1969, about forty students marching under the banner of People's Democracy left Belfast in Northern Ireland. Outside Derry on 4 January their way was blocked by Unionists at Burntollet Bridge, leading to a riot of historic proportions. Soon Northern Ireland was in the grips of civil strife. Immediately following this turmoil tourism to Ireland came to an abrupt stop and went into a permanent decline.

By now, I had remembered 'the marriage question' and wedding plans were in their advanced stages. In February of that year and while still in a state of euphoria, Ann and I were married. The day went off very well, but as soon as possible we left for London and the Canary Islands. Now comes the part that I don't recommend to any groom. My devoted buddy Johnny Lee, the Aer Lingus pilot, suggested I should take the surfboard. Ann reluctantly agreed even though she now was going to have to share her honeymoon with a third party! On our first day at the main beach in Las Palmas, I managed to catch a few peaks close to shore before the tide got too high. Ann was glad of this because at least now she and I could pad around the town and merge with locals. Then with a hired sports car and with the board jammed in just like I did in Hawaii, we drove the forty miles south to Maspalomas. It was there that I got in a lot of small fast nasty waves and met a host of guys that we both knew from Jersey, who were there for the winter.

One day one of the Jersey fellows saw a kid take his board, and ran frantically to stop him. Unfortunately, his foot went into one of many holes in the flat rocky formation bordering the shore, and he broke his leg. His friends immediately brought him to the airport and sent him home. We guessed he had no medical insurance for Spain or, as they said, the care would not be up to the UK standard! The following day my luck also ran out. I tried to catch a shoulder-high wave, and somehow paddled so hard that the board twirled around on take-off, and the fin sliced into my foot. Now this was no ordinary fin; it was the long dagger fin on the South African board that I had bought in Tramore. This was justice being done for bringing the board, do you agree? Ann certainly did! I reckon God forgives, but nature gets even.

Irish Surfing Association Formation 1969–70

In July of that year, Neil Armstrong and Buzz Aldrin landed on the moon, demonstrating to the citizens of our planet that the sky was the limit. Optimism was at an all-time high – what a wonderful world! Brian Britton was now studying economics at Trinity College Dublin, with the ultimate ambition of becoming an accountant. So, on a dark winter's evening in October, and after several phone calls to the different clubs to discuss an association, Harry, Roger, Dave Kenny and I drove to the centre of the city and parked without difficulty almost in front of the college. God be with the days! Brian was resident in 'rooms' and happily opened a cream-painted door for us, saying at the same time,

'Welcome, lads. I am stashed here for the next year or two – economics, accountancy, commerce, you know!'

We entered the room. Brian had a conference table laid out in the centre and so we took our places.

'Hope I'm not too young to be involved in serious planning, you know I'm just a student,' said Brian.

The purpose of the meeting was to create an association and we needed Brian's input. Bo Vance from Belfast had already given his blessing to the meeting but could not manage the trip. We agreed that to form a useful association we would need people like Brian and Dave, who had their livelihoods by the sea. We also recognised that Brian lived in a place where the sport was blossoming, By contrast, my Dad's hotel was on the wrong side of the country; it had been a base for me to set things rolling, but that was during the age of innocence. So we agreed that we should call it the Irish Surfing Association, get a letterhead printed, and request submissions for the drawing up of our constitution.

Further meetings were held in the Purty Kitchen pub in Dun Laoghaire, at which the small print was worked out. The story goes that Dave, while taking minutes, spied a pretty girl at the bar with a friend. When the friend went to the washroom, Dave darted over and got her name and phone number, as he had seen her briefly once before. She was later to become his wife.

In Early 1970, there was a final meeting for the official formation of the Irish Surfing Association – ISA. This meeting began and ended when we finally got agreement from all the clubs about how the organisation would function. I was given the honorary position of first president, Brian became chairman, Bo Vance, vice-chairman, Roger became secretary and Harry became treasurer.

One year later more clubs wanted representation on the committee, and the posts rotated. Brian then became president, a position that he held for some thirty-three years, till he retired in 2003. As an accountant Brian therefore knew exactly how to make ventures have a successful bottom line. To him that meant surfing would have to have benefactors, sponsors and political contacts of the fibre that would build the sport for the future. Taking a peek into that future, one finds that Roci Allan from the Rossnowlagh Surf Club was voted onto the ISA committee. Roci and Brian between them negotiated a property in Easkey, Co. Sligo and made it an HQ for the association.

Then a permanent secretary was appointed. This was Zoe Lally, a previous Irish Women's Surfing Champion and a legal professional by trade. She was the ideal person, who could combine her surfing experience with the administration necessary for such a body. Her calm, measured approach, blended with a love for the sport and credentials to prove it, made her the 'Yoda' and cornerstone of the sport on the island.

St Patrick's Weekend

Letting out a laugh, Hughie O'Brien Moran recalled a trip to Lahinch along with his brother Niall:

'I was just remembering probably March 1970 when a Surf Club of Ireland surfari weekend was organised to Lahinch. Our cousin Frank O'Mahony from Limerick and I were in the group. We stayed at the newly built Liscannor Hotel, and were probably among its first customers. We all met at the hotel and I was sitting with a group which included Harry Evans. He was drinking a large bottle of Phoenix. Being new to beer, and looking at the way he was relishing it, I decided to have the same. I couldn't believe how awful it tasted and kept watching Harry to see if he was flinching. With great difficulty I persisted, and by the second bottle it didn't seem so bad. By the end of the night I was very enthusiastic about

Phoenix as we all euphorically played 'ring a ring a roses' in the bar.' He continued;

'The next morning Chuck Conklin came back from Lahinch declaring the waves to be to twenty feet, and offshore. Kevin and I battled our way outside, and though I can't remember catching any waves, just getting out was a big achievement. On mature reflection, the waves were probably a quarter the size of Chuck's original estimate, but that didn't stop us from feeling like heroes. Later we all surfed the beach at the Liscannor end. It was a great weekend at a time when all surfers felt very close.'

For the record, Chuck Conklin was a US Navy diver who was commissioned by Gregg Bemis, an American millionaire, to dive on the wreck of the *Lusitania* at the Old Head of Kinsale. He explained to Ann and me one evening in Kinsale that he had to breathe helium when diving deep. He descends regularly to the wreck to salvage what they request and he said they had a special interest in its screws. This daunting task had us agog, not to mention the fact that, when in Lahinch, he had an endless capacity to go out in enormous waves.

Hugh then told us:

'Frank O'Mahony pointed out to me years later what good value the hotel had been. We paid something like three pounds, seventeen shillings and sixpence for the weekend's bed, breakfast and an evening banquet. £.s.d. was the currency at the time, just before decimal currency arrived and the decline of the old empires!'

In that same year, 1970, in Strandhill the young Tom Hickey was trying out his talents as a surfer and quickly after that made his mark as a competitive surfer and lifeguard. As he was so fit his surfing developed in leaps, bounds and fast turns. Alongside Willie Parks and Gene Parks, Tom was one of two new disciples (the other being Stan Burns), who would help revolutionise surfing in the north-west by using a smaller-than-average board. Stan originally used Willie Parks's ten-foot Bilbo board that he had bought from C&S in '66. On this board he learned to stand, turn and develop his appetite for the waves. Then bought an eight-foot-six Bilbo and with that purchase he said his surfing went forward another leap. Stan earned money to surf by playing jazz music at night and telling the audience all about the merits of Strandhill and its secret weapon – surfing.

In the summer of that same year I was lucky with first place in the newly presented Limerick Leader contest, presented by Mrs Wright, one of the owners of the newspaper. On the following year, I did not do so well. The 1971 results were; Derek Musgrave from Tramore first, I got second, and Brian Cusack of Limerick third. Getting second place was probably because I goofed up by dropping in on a guy and was docked points. In the early days, dropping in had hardly been noticed but now it was seen as a serious transgression. This proved that point I had not read the small print, or keep up with the times.

C&S Showroom

We finally got a mortgage for a bungalow, which in those days took nearly nine months to be granted. It was a basic bungalow with the added feature of a ow-pitched roof that overhung the front door giving it a ranch effect. We named it Susswald, which we thought meant 'Sweetwood' in German. As it turned out, süss means sweet-tasting, and was not the correct adjective to use. However, we liked the sound and let it remain. There was a steep slope down to a millrace behind the house. So that we could get down the slope, I built steps and a platform where one could sit. This platform was made from – what do you know? It was my second original stand-up surfboard, * one that was sheared of its foam on Magheramore beach years beforehand. There was a spare room at the side of the house with a separate entrance. All the newly imported boards were stored there. In order to make it more professional, Roger constructed a wooden rack that could hold almost twenty at a time. The room became bedecked with boards and O'Neill wetsuits, thereby becoming Ireland's first surf shop!

It was always tempting to try out some of the additional items, such as a new-style wetsuit with the zip on the back. On one occasion, I tried this wetsuit on a lonely beach, and when I got back to dry land I discovered the zip was stuck. It was getting dark and I was chilled and needed to get out of the suit. Therefore, I drove in haste to the nearest garage in Wicklow Town, some five miles away, and asked to be cut free. The salesman refused but directed me to a mechanic who knew just what to do!

When boards were delivered into the docks at Dublin, Wicklow or Arklow, we would have to borrow my Dad's van to collect the consignment. The excitement of surfing and providing boards and wetsuits gave Roger and I, a profound sense of purpose, and a little cash on the side. Now we also began to trade-in used boards for new. This meant more and more surfing, paddling or even being towed behind anyone who would agree. We got some good photos of wake surfing in Greystones on a clear sunny day in June. One can see the rope being let go as the free riding begin.

Amazingly, In 2009, I was phoned by the then owners of Susswald to say that they had discovered the old board. With thanks and appreciation, I refurbished it as close as possible to its original form and in 2007 donated it to the T Bay S.C. Sadly, since then Susswald has been sold and demolished to make way for six new houses. An end room in Susswald had a separate entrance and in the sixties, this was our C&S surf shop – the first in Ireland. Many years later a friend told me Susswald had been demolished to make way for new houses. One of the new occupants is Ireland's women champion boxers.

Jersey Again

In 1970 the world was an exciting place. Paul McCartney took court proceedings that broke up the Beatles as a performing group, Jimmy Hendrix mysteriously died, Biafra surrendered after a 32-month fight for independence from Nigeria. Rhodesia severed its last tie with the British Crown and declared itself a racially segregated republic. US troops invaded Cambodia, four students at Kent State University in Ohio were slain by National Guardsmen at a demonstration protesting the incursion into Cambodia and in the surfing world it was business as usual, with the continuous building of shorter, lighter boards to ride larger waves than ever before.

In September the Irish, who were now competitive surfers, entered an international event to be held in Jersey. Soon after arrival Dave Prichard of the British Surfing Association approached us and said,

'Would you consider Ireland hosting the next European Championships in 1972? You are welcome to it.'

We were astounded, and replied to the poignant question, 'Dave, are you quite serious? I did not think we are advanced enough to do that!'

'Sure, you are! Talk to your people and just let me know.'

I knew there and then that we would agree, despite the prospects of a year of very hard work.

On our return, we had the joy of another contest. It was the 1970 Tramore event, the third they had hosted so far. Hugh O'Brien-Moran got first and Derek Musgrave got third. The sea was much like the other two events held there, but the surfing was vastly different. Boards were now quite thick, wide and short, measuring about seven feet, six inches on average. This allowed for very radical manoeuvres and was of great spectator value. Amongst the internationals were Gordon Burgis and Norman Redman from

Wales. Norman, known as Nobby, arranged a memorial photo with twenty-four of the participants which shows clearly the styles, the faces and the boards used in those far-off days.

The while at the third Intercounty event in October 1970, and while photographing the contest with my old Pentax Spotmatic, someone said,

'Haello, what's happening here? Is that surfing out there?'

I turned and saw a middle aged American with an inquisitive smile.

I replied, 'Yeah, sir that is surfing. What part of Canada or the States are you from?'

'Montauk, Long Island,' he said.

I gulped, and then opened up - telling him all about Tom Casey who was drafted and never heard of again.

'Well, my boy, if you give me your address I will check him out when I get home and let you know.'

So that was done, and six months later I got a letter to say poor Tom had been killed in a helicopter accident in Vietnam. Later they found out his chopper was hit and ammunition on board exploded. Tom Casey, RIP, was the first casualty of Irish Surfing. In later years Erick Randal from California, while working for T Bay Surf Club, located Tom's US Army memorial for anyone who is interested:

www.thewall-usa.com/guest.asp?recid=8311

So why not locate this memorial, and post a thank-you to Tom for his early contribution to the formation of the sport.

When the event ended the competitors were invited into Vinnie and family's new Surfers Bar. This was decorated with old boards and photos of the earlier years. Already the past six years had become history. The bar's collection of memorabilia was to grow with time, till the walls became covered with pictures of great events up to this very day. Part of the fun was the live music and dancing provided on the two evenings of the event. Barry Britton was always a fixture as he stood for hours on end with his grisly beard and healthy pint, while he chatted to one and all. His brother Conor, as Barry said, always made sure the kegs were empty before the hotel closed for the winter. Then the surfers got to dance, jump around and hug the life out of one another, especially if of opposite gender.

Aloha Ka Hoa

The phone rang. It was Roger, and he sounded strained.

'Do you remember I said I might be transferred overseas in the near future? Well, it's happened; I am going to Kuala Lumpur next month.'

'Oh no, Roger,' I blurted. 'That's terrible for us, but wonderful for you and the family – wishing you lots of luck.'

Then he added, 'That means we will have to demolish our C&S Surfboards business. I will come over to the store in Susswald and we can share out the boards between us.'

I agreed, and sadly we removed the bounty from Roger's fabulous surf rack and divided the spoils.

Shortly after that, we had a farewell dinner for the Steadman's in the roof-top restaurant of our hotel. It was held on Friday 27th November 1970. Dress was informal, tickets cost 32 shillings and 6 pence (or £1-12-6). Mike Murphy and Sam McCrum arranged for many of the Lahinch crowd to attend, because their friendship with Roger and Rosemary. The Surf Club of Ireland presented them with an oil painting of the misty hills of Donegal, and Harry Evans made a moving speech. He mentioned how Roger had overcome all the obstacles of relocating in our tiny isle of Celts, and at the same time won our hearts. Then he said, not only had Roger done that, but much more by putting Ireland on the world surfing stage. With lumps in our throats, the group bade Roger and Rosemary goodbye and they departed for the orient. These were the first of the wild geese to leave the country, but more would follow in the near future and that would stall the development of surfing for a short period.

Now the newly introduced Value Added Tax (VAT) became liable at point of entry to the country, so there would never have been a future for our business, unless we had gone into it full time. VAT would have jeopardised our very informal activity, based on a minimum of paperwork and maximum of enjoyment. No other equation would be worth the trouble. That was the end of importing Bilbo boards and the automatic ending of the agency. It was necessary to arrange to send legal papers to Roger to sign and return after retaining a copy. The reason for this is that until that is done all parties who act in business together are automatically liable for each other's debts. This information from our accountant came as a surprise and had to be obeyed. The signed documents now removed mutual liability. This might have been an act of over-caution, but who knows?

CHAPTER 13

European Event in France 1971

In July 1971, The Limerick Leader newly presented cup was won by Derek Musgrave. The Europeans were held that October 1971, at Seignosse Le Penon ne Hossegor in south-west France. Once again, we got an enthusiastic team together, conveyed into battle with three cars. One came from Tramore with Dave and Paul Kenny and Eamon Matthews, while another came from Lahinch with Sam McCrum, Wally Fogarty and his brother, and from Wicklow there was Ann and me. We now drove a 1968 Opel Record station wagon. This car was the ideal surf-mobile – long, with a hatchback, and navy-blue in colour.

The three expeditions converged on Rosslare at around the same time, all intent on catching the ferry to Le Havre. As Ann and I arrived, my clutch hit the floor – it had collapsed! As this happened at the top of the hill approaching the dock, we freewheeled down the hill and arrived at the back of the line of cars going on the ferry. I scurried up to the check-in desk and told them of our plight. As luck had it, there was an AA man standing there, and he looked at our AA insurance papers and said that no garage could fix it in time.

However, he added, 'Why don't we tow you on board, and you can get it fixed in France on your insurance. After all, you are already in transit.'

I almost choked with delight. Just then the Limerick car arrived. Wally and Sam sauntered up the line and talked in our window, wondering why we were stopped dead. When they heard the news, they chuckled and Wally said,

'Look, we have the trunk filled with spare parts to cover any breakdown or eventuality.'

Then they wished us luck and said as they drove past, 'See you in on board!'

They were roaring laughing and drawing fingers across their throats. We enjoyed the male cynicism even though we were the butt of the humour. It seems at that stage the other car with the Tramore boys was already on the ferry. Then as the last car drove up the ramp, the AA man, true to his word, had us towed on to the ship. As we pulled out of Rosslare we met an enormous sea and learned that it was just short of stopping the crossing altogether.

This was young Paul Kenny's first trip away, and he was enchanted by the experience, and by the size of sea. He just stayed on deck glued to the rail, gazing at each approaching wall of water. Soon we all gathered with him, as the waves bearing down on the ship hit it with mighty impact. Each wave smashed across the foredeck and a great shudder went through the hull – not a time for sleeping!

Next morning, we arrived in Le Havre and said adios to the two carloads of eager beavers who were to carry on without us. 'See you in Seignosse,' they taunted, as they speed off down '*la route*'. When all the cars and everyone had departed the stevedores came toward us like a bunch of terrorists getting ready for the kill. Then, with a jolt, they pushed us off the boat, shut up the ramp, and we were left all alone in a huge empty car park, and going nowhere. So, armed with an address, I set off and located the garage which did AA work.

We spent a pleasant night in Le Havre and by 1 p.m. the following day the car was ready. Once on the road the incident was quickly forgotten. Then, distracted by the French bread, cheese and vino, we stopped and started, and stopped again. We loved France but also wondered how our amigos were getting on.

Mike Murphy, then the Hon. Secretary of the West Coast Surf Club, recalled:

'The journey started on a most exciting note, to see Kevin Cavey's car being towed on board the ferry minus a clutch. Just after leaving Le Havre we also had a misadventure because we got a puncture and had visions of Kevin passing us by, waving and laughing out the window. However, that did not happen because once it was mended we took a more direct route to Seignosse and felt sure he would go by a different route, which he did. When eventually we got there, we were overcome by the great waves and wonderful surfing standards being demonstrated.'

The Irish Team in Seignosse, France 1971. Top left – Niall and Hugh, O'Brian Moran, Paul Kenny. Lower left, Derek Mc Crum, Brian Cusack, Kevin Cavey, Sammy Mc Crum and Wally Fogarty

When Ann and I got to Seignosse, like all contestants we were accommodated at 'Village Vacances Famille', which was a sort of Club Med, at the cost of ten shillings equivalent per night, because this was a camp for French social welfare people on holiday. It was a very South-Sea-island-looking dwelling, with a high, pointed roof sloping down to tropical vegetation and all open-sided. It was laid out around tennis courts and close to a barrier of monstrous golden sand dunes. The dining was communal but very enjoyable when one was ravenous after a day in the sea. There were lavish open-sided lounges where I enjoyed smoking a cigar after dinner. The weather was clear, sunny and very warm. At night, we could hear the boom of the very large surf hitting the beach and reminding us of what was to come!

Next day, we were up at dawn, and enjoyed coffee with French bread that was hung in a bag on the doorknob. We then hurried to the beach, meeting our pals sleepily heading in the same direction. The scene was just what a surf contest should look like: flags, tanned surfers, cool chicks and enormous waves. By now I had shed the African-made board and had a new, very thick, buoyant, seven-foot-six-inch Bilbo board. I really felt comfortable with that sort of board construction, and got the feeling I could take on anything. When you have a good board that is how you should feel, otherwise there is something wrong.

The Irish team paddled out to warm up, shake off the beer and wine, and learn some French slang for 'my wave'. Though the waves came in beautiful straight lines and looked easy to handle, that was not the case! Firstly, they were six feet plus, and the clean-up sets were ten feet. This was one of the reasons why it took almost twenty minutes for most of us to struggle outside. The tide was low and the impact zone was generally in chest-deep water, so the crunch was violent. These waves were also so hollow that on that first occasion the whiplash left me deafened for quite a while.

Soon, the contest began and as usual we as a team did our best, but with guys like Gordon Burgis, Tigger Newling, Graham Nile and Mick Wingfield as opposition, it was an uphill struggle for the children of Danann. However, our guys needed some encouragement because at one point one of the team said he was not getting in as the surf was too big. We could not force him. I tried getting a bit tough with him but again the bloke refused. Then the plague spread! Another fellow said he wasn't getting in because he hated seaweed. Ann agreed with his whim. So, despite my urgings, again the bloke refused.

Just competing in this event was uplifting. It was Hugh O'Brien-Moran who did the best of us all by qualifying for the quarter-finals. Hugh had developed a taste for tackling the biggest waves he could find. He was the guy who looked like he had Polynesian ancestors, and salt water for blood – he just thrived on big surf. Now, armed with camera and long lens, I got a few shots of him in action. We relied on Hughie to carry the flag for the Emerald Isle, and that he did. The organisers also asked Ann to judge, and as she had done it before, she agreed. So, she was place with the other judges on a very high podium overlooking the splendid surf scene to mark her card. I got a good photo of her in a straw hat doing that task in blazing sunshine and saying, 'Vive la France!'

The results of the Championships were, in winning order: England, France, Jersey, Spain, and fifth was Hugh O'Brien-Moran for Ireland, follow by Wales and Guernsey. Chris Jones of England won the individual prize.

One interesting development was the formation of the European Surfing Federation and their looking forward to the Europeans being held the following year in Lahinch. After the contest was concluded we scampered off to surf at La Barre. This beach is at the mouth of the Adour River at Bayonne, just north of Biarritz. Where the river enters the sea, there is a long sea wall protruding into the bay. As one might expect, this wall creates a side-wash effect and coupled with silt and sand seabed, great wave are formed. Therefore, the beach shelves and the surf breaks with a lot of power but close to shore. By now we were accustomed to size and everyone got outside easily and caught rides, but getting out afterwards was a more difficult task because of the amount of backwash. Sammy took some great rides with vertical drop-ins, while Hugh just laughed as he glided across peeling sections with the ease of a seagull in flight.

Ann Cavey, judging at the European 1971, Seignosse le Penon

When the visit to paradise was over, and we eventually returned to La Havre, one car was missing. It was Limerick's battlewagon that had allegedly brought all the equipment needed for unforeseen repairs. Wally and Mike sent word that they were delayed due to a clutch failure and that they did not have a spare part to solve such a major problem. We heard later that they had to leave the car in France, with boards on top, and retrieve it at another time. At Rosslare, the customs were alert and asked me if I had bought tyres in France. They knew something had happened but in all honesty, I answered no, and hoped that they would not ask about repairs. They did not ask and I was able to drive on home.

On our return, I was told that there had been some dissension about forcing the frightened member of the team to surf. After that, I reckoned that the world was going downhill, and changing from soft to just plain mushy.

Hillsville and Lahinch

This was unfamiliar territory for most of the gang. It was April, and we were going to converge from all corners of Ireland at the Hillsville Hotel near Castlegregory on the Dingle Peninsula. Ann and I had got the loan of a small caravan and towed it there.

The weather was very wet and the entrance to the property was overhung with trees and quite eerie – like entering Gravesend Manor. The hotel itself was grey and foreboding and it had a large damp conservatory and some newish bedrooms in an extension to one side. We drew up on an unkempt lawn and unhitched our caravan; it had been agreed with the hotel that some people would camp there. In no time, other members arrived and erected tents. Alan Duke, Davie Govan and some others were squashed under the canvas, and immediately dug into a binge of cornflakes. Some of the club smoothies booked into the hotel, but most people just camped in the ever-increasing rain. Among the more established surfers there were Tony Gleeson and Dermot Hughes, both with their wives. That night there was a great singsong with a fellow in US Army Vietnam-style swamp boots playing the guitar and singing Neil Diamond's 'Song Sung Blue':

'Song sung blue, everybody knows one.

Song sung blue, every garden grows one.'

Next morning, after Alan and the boys had devoured more cornflakes, the group headed off to the beach. Just then, through the mist, a small car arrived. It was the Byrnes from Bray who, as soon as they reached driving age, commandeered their parents'

Mini Cooper, stashed their boards on top, and headed for Castlegregory. They were wearing Beatle-style clothes and very long hair when they arrived. My tiny daughter Carolyn lit up and squealed, 'Look, the Wombles.'

These Wombles were already very good surfers. As this was their first surfari, I introduced them to the group. As it turned out, the surf was varied but not very easy to ride, while over in Inch it was equally difficult and smaller, and the point of the promontory, Coumeenoole, was blown out. Thus, between beer, cornflakes, rain and sea, it was just one liquid weekend, especially for the campers. However, some of the group did find a wave or two to their liking.

Murf, from the West Coast Surf Club, had a story and some humour to add:

'First stop was at the beautiful little beach of Coumeenoole as featured in the film Ryan's Daughter. However, the tide was in fully in and gave little in the way of waves. From there we proceeded to Inch via the Conor Pass, which featured some beautiful scenery. I'm sure we met about twenty-five access roads and took the fifth one, and after tearing through farmyards with wild abandon to the sound of screaming chickens and flying feathers, the road stopped on the sand and about forty feet from some very good surf. Sam and I quickly took to the water and got the hang of riding four-foot walls to the right and being prepared for it all to heave over in the last few seconds. But it was fun!'

That just about concluded the Castlegregory adventure and all people wanted to know was, 'What's next?'

On July 15th, 1972, the Limerick Leader Cup was run once again in Lahinch by the West Coast Surf Club. The cup was large and generous in design. It was run in midsummer when the weather was usually at its warmest. The Limerick Leader newspaper wrote that this event would decide who might be on the Irish team for the forthcoming European Surfing Championships scheduled for

September next. This was true, but of more importance, it was going to an opportunity to get in a bit of enjoyable surfing. I thought that if there were good waves, it could be a memorable contest.

It turned out just as desired; the waves were about head-high, well-shaped, and with only a light onshore wind. I had two days surfing Lahinch before the event and felt very confident. We had gone there on the Wednesday before the event and I had got in a lot of surfing, which helped wash the previous month's hotel static out of my system. As luck had it, but also to my surprise, I won the event and was presented with the cup by Mrs J.F. Wright of the Limerick Leader newspaper. A photo of this was taken in which the onlookers included Ann and Dave Kenny's mother, while to the left of the picture there was Derek Musgrave of Tramore in second place and to the right Paul Kenny, also from Tramore, who got third.

It was around that year that we presented the Royal Starlight Hotel Novice Cup – obviously for beginners, while at the same time there was the new Liscannor Cup, both of which also were run in the Lahinch locality.

All this and other razzmatazz helped put surfing on the map in

CHAPTER 14

European Championships Lahinch, 1972

The 1972 World Championships had just been held in San Diego and Ireland was not represented, mainly because we had our own contest challenges to meet. The San Diego winning names were: 1st, James Blears (Hawaii); 2nd, David Nuuhiwa (USA); 3rd, Peter Townend (Australia). Surfing was beginning to turn professional, and this was the last world amateur championships. Word had it that future results would focus on the growing professional circuit rather than one event.

1 Frank O Mahony Limerick
2 Alan Mustwin Wales
3 Brian Britton Donegal
4 Pat Cunningham Tramore
5 Nobby. Norman Redmon Wales
6 Conor Britton Donegal
7 John Boomer N.Ireland
8 Alan Duke N.Ireland
9 Ted Alexandro N.Ireland
10 Tom O Brien Cork
11 Tom O Connor Cork
12 Alan Rich Surfer Mag.
13 Barry Rose Cork
14 Dave Kenny Tramore
15 Toby S. Africa
16 Don O Sullivan Cork
17 John O Brien Tramore
18 Jane? Liked bad guitar playing
19 Dave Moynan
20 Kevin Cavey. One of the first Irish surfers
21 Gordon Burgess Jersey
22 Tigger Newling Cornwall
23 Hugh O Brien Moran Tramore (He loved my stews)
24 Jane Cross Cork

Nobby Redman
n4norm@gmail.com
Tramore Ireland 1972

Tramore 1972. Photo by Norman (Noddy) Redmond

In the north-west, things were on the move, as Stan Burns and Tom Hickey had begun to surf Strandhill. They were both very eager and had the advantage of being able to start with seven- and eight-foot boards. This meant they could climb and drop and cut back with ease – something the old boys struggled to achieve. Tom was fiercely competitive but his first priority was to qualify as a schoolteacher. What student would ever believe that their teacher was a real live surfer? In Tramore a new protégé, Henry Moore, was beginning to show he too was a 'Metal Man', as his standard of surfing was winning him local contests. Henry's height and powerful physique was his greatest asset.

However, things were also heating up in Co. Clare. The spirit of fun, frolic and practical jokes were the hallmarks of the West Coast Surf Club. Wherever they went, there was always fun, fun, fun. The Tramore Club members were just about as jolly, always ready to get up and stomp around the dance floor, or just jump around, wherever there was music. All this added soul to the sport and attracted other young vibrant youth to the cause. Murf the Surf tells us more:

'In 1972, our fun-loving club introduced a trophy called the 'Perpetual Priceless Plastic Brontosaurus Turd'. This sophisticated title is quite deceiving as the trophy was no more than a chunk of plastic, washed onto the beach along with driftwood. So as to attract competitors they even ran a late people's heat, but people were even late for that!'

Now for the serious side of things; a steering committee had been formed to set planning in motion for the hosting of the 1972 European Surfing Championships in Lahinch. The date selected was September 16th, a time when the waves are usually good. After much discussion, the management team was formed up and began its work. From the east coast there was Harry Evans, our ex-military man, who was appointed as contest manager and chairman in charge of team heats and general preparations, and I was to look after public relations. Brian Britton from Rossnowlagh was treasurer and secretary and Grant Robinson his assistant. Conor Britton was head judge. From Tramore there was Dr O'Brien-Moran and D. Giles, who both who dealt with team enquiries and general assistance. From Cork there was D. O'Reilly, and Tom Flynn, who looked after the scoring and, so as to perfect this process, constructed a magnificent scoreboard. He brought the board with him all the way from Cork and then proceeded to assemble it outside the surf centre. He was assisted by Jane Cross, Frank McEnnis and Tom O'Brien, representatives from Cork.

From Lahinch, there was Sammy McCrum, the jester and spirit of the organisation, who volunteered as beach marshal and the Clare-to-Donegal international surfari organiser. There was P.J. Clearihan, who had worked on all the contests so far and assisted Tom Flynn with the score auditing. Michael Murphy and his girlfriend Henrietta looked after the teams' accommodation in hotels and guesthouses. Other support came from Frank McEnnis and Brian Cusack, with assistance from such characters as Pip Cullen, Brian Dixon, Eddie Comber, Barry Drinnan, Dea Hedden, Kevin Neagle, Hugh Milne, John Wright, John

O'Connell, Des Deeney and Antoin O'Looney, who eventually bought a magnificent hostelry overlooking the best surfing section of Lahinch beach. John Guinan, who was both from Lahinch and Dublin, remembers:

Welsh team, contest winners and below, Vivienne
Evans and Jane Cross, Euro '72

'I usually went to Lahinch while on visits to Limerick for the weekend and at most there would be five in the water. The only people in Dublin I knew at that time were the Byrnes in Bray – we used to try and find surf at Bray Head and Arklow – also tried Magheramore but never got it working properly.'

Dr O'Brien Moran said that Lahinch was originally chosen as a venue because of the large generous facilities it had to offer, along with proximity to Shannon Airport.

Michael Vaughan of Shannonside Tourism became more and more interested in the sport as time went on. He noticed the upturn in accommodation in the area when the surfers were in town. Lahinch had golfing as its main attraction, but another string to the bow would do no harm. Acting as a mentor to surfing, he made sure that any grants going would be put in our direction. He was to Lahinch as Dr O'Brien-Moran had been to Tramore. The rules of the event permitted various team sizes as follows:

England 10 (juniors 4) France 8 (juniors 3) Jersey 8 (juniors 3)

Spain 6 (juniors 3) Guernsey 6 (juniors 3) Ireland 6 (juniors 3)

Wales 6 (juniors 3) Scotland 2 (juniors 1) Total 52 (juniors 23)

On the England team, there were previous champions like Chris Jones, and Don Garsden from Essex, Neil Wright and Jerry Peake, Newquay, and Tim Heyland, North Devon, the man who came to Ireland right after Rodney Sumpter had visited. England also had Graham Nile, the current UK champion, Mick Wingfield, Pete Bounds, Roger Mansfield and Keith Beddoe. Surfing for Jersey there was Gordon Burgis, among others. There were also teams from Scotland, Wales, France, Spain and, of course, Ireland. Naturally there were visiting Australians and Americans who got to help with the beach marshalling and encouraging us all in our chores. Unfortunately, Rodney Sumpter could not be there due to his prior accident. We missed his vitality and charm, and also missed Roger Steadman, who had already departed to Malaysia.

'My name is Peter Kennerley from RTÉ, and I'm here to make a film about the European Surfing Championships.'

A thin man in his mid-fifties or early sixties stood with his hand extended in a gesture of friendship. He was thin and wiry and partial to a glass of Irish whiskey, as I found out. As public relations person, I took Peter to meet the competitors and film where he liked. Then Peter said he would like to film me alone in the dunes with the waves breaking in the background. As it turned out, only Doughmore, now known as Doonbeg Beach, fitted his requirements. He took shots of me dressed in a khaki shirt and blue jeans striding up the dunes and looking out to sea. This got included in some newsreels along with his meticulous report on the contest.

On the big day, 16th September, to our dismay the waves were small, and thousands of spectators witnessed our plight. Despite this, the contest got massive coverage because it was the only sporting event happening in the country that weekend. It was the only event that could possibly happen in the face of a terrible political situation in the north of Ireland and its spillover effects on the south. The dissatisfaction by the Republican minority had led to violence, bombings and atrocities from both sides. All this was getting world media coverage – not good for tourism in Lahinch or even Bray. Now here was a sport that defied all the norms and welcomed UK teams with open arms while holding sport over all other considerations. Most people felt that surfing well deserved the good coverage that was now being provided.

Therefore, after consultation with the visiting teams, our contest management decided it was all systems go! Though the waves remained small for both days, by Sunday 17th the finals were run. The audience became intrigued by the activities and the acrobatics at sea. Small waves now became a source of great entertainment and lack of size was overlooked.

The team results were, in winning order: England 38 points, Wales 35, France 31, Jersey 30, Ireland 27, and Spain 18.

The team junior results were: France 33 points, Wales 27, England 26, Ireland 12, and Spain 10.

Junior individual results were: D. Halpin (Wales) 148 points, D. Daladdie (France) 122, and S. Daniel (England) 133.

The best individual wave taken by a junior was B. Cadepont for France.

The final day was enhanced by a shoal of dolphins that appeared behind Paul Kenny while he was surfing across a well-formed wave. We got a photo and footage of the incident for posterity. So, with all that said and done, it was now time to recognise the team achievements – let there be a celebration!

After a mammoth banquet in the Sports Centre, Harry Evans thanked the members of the Lahinch Development Association, and congratulated them for the wonderful work they had put into the event; without their co-operation and the use of the entertainment complex, the Championships could never have been staged. He then went on to thank Mr Michael O'Kennedy, Parliamentary Secretary to the Minister for Education, for opening the event on the first day and for kindly attending its closure. After that it was a big thank-you to the teams and to the event committee and supportive clubs. Lastly, he singled out Michael Vaughan for being a friend to surfing from its infancy, even though most of the surfers were now in the process of overcoming their infancy. There was a big laugh.

Then there was a great disco in the ballroom at the centre that continued into the wee hours. Looking back, one person stood out, and it was the young and vibrant Steve Daniels from Cornwall, who in later years would return for a great celebration – the fortieth year of Irish surfing. This was to be a great gathering of pilgrims from the distant past – the very people who took part on this weekend – the 1972 Europeans!

Mike Murphy, recalls the trials of organising the Championships from ground level up:

'Looking back on the two days and the preceding nine months, I think we felt that it was worth the effort. The many hours of argument, discussion and organisation, the hundreds of phone calls, the many nights spent travelling to venues for meetings and home again at all hours; the frustrating attempts to secure a big commercial sponsor, the challenging work in getting press coverage, radio and TV, the coaxing of foreign teams to participate against a background of political turmoil – was all worthwhile. Many acts of appreciation were noted when each team came personally to thank the committee for their work but particularly when the French team made the lack of surf on Sunday seem quite trivial.'

The next day, Monday 18th, we noticed plumes of water breaking over at Bartra Point. This was a sign that something was happening down the coast. We did not have the web in those days, and we forecast waves according to the wind or what could be seen. The French team had unfortunately departed for home but elements from all the remaining teams loaded up to do what they do best – seek out waves.

We headed south towards Spanish Point and to our delight discovered a reef (now called the inside reef) breaking in glassy conditions and well over head-height. About thirty warriors strode across a field, and then clambered over the rocks and paddled out to this mysterious unknown break. As I was one of the first there, I gingerly paddled out not sure of what lay beneath. As the waves were well overhead there must have been enough depth between the trough of the wave and the bottom. Perhaps five feet at least. I caught an early wave on my seven-foot-six Bilbo. I went right, and enjoyed the acceleration as the wave exploded behind me. After a few such rides, things got difficult as it became crowded. From here on only the really experienced guys like Chris Jones, Alan Duke and Davie Govan would master the break. Those wizards got some great rides with lots of whoops of appreciation from the onlookers. In the holy words of 'Murf':

'There was a bus arranged to take the English team to the airport for a 3.30 p.m. flight. As word had got around that there was surf in Spanish Point half of the team went there, leaving the bus waiting. Once there, they unsheathed their boards and joined the Welsh, Spanish and Irish who had got there first. Our eyes were opened when we saw our visitors carve up some waves that were peaking up to ten feet. On the local front, Kevin Neagle surfed magnificently, never missing any wave that came his way.

'Then I said to Brian Cusack that we just must get in. As I paddled out on my board with no leash, an enormous set arrived and as I tried to climb up its face and over the back, I got caught by the breaking lip. It was at that moment that my enthusiasm for surfing took a downgrade, because I was catapulted over and backwards, and plunged to the rock bottom, not once but twice. Ha, ha, Brian said, not realising what a close encounter of the third kind I had just experienced.'

Then as the tide rose the waves stopped breaking and there were just walls that fizzled out. We all came in one by one as frustration set in, but one guy remained. As we changed into clothes a mammoth set suddenly appeared. It was so big that it was definitely going to break, and break it did! The lone surfer was in the right place at the right time and he paddled with confidence and took an enormous drop, riding it over the reef and all the way to the rocky shore. This ride got an ovation from all and ride saved him having to paddle in. Barry Britton recalls:

'I was sixteen when Euro surf 1972 hit Lahinch in County Clare. The surf was crap but the partying was magnificent. The Thursday before the contest I witnessed something extraordinary and it has stayed with me ever since. Looking out to sea at outer Spanish Point all I could see were specks moving across the faces of huge waves, leaving a white trail behind them. Not only were these the biggest waves I had ever seen ridden, they were doing it over rocks! It turned out that it was Davy Govan and Alan Duke from the north coast and they were putting on a command performance for us awestruck gremmies standing on the rocky shoreline.

'Now bearing that in mind, on the Monday after the contest I knew exactly where we should go – back to that same place. Therefore, we headed for that inside reef at Spanish Point which turned out to be running at six feet and glassy. This would be a welcome relief from the poor surf during the contest and at least some of the visiting teams would benefit.

'It seems that almost everyone from the contest had paddled out to the reef so I also had a go. Davy witnessed my first ride over rocks on my first short board of eight foot, and was bursting himself laughing at the look of absolute fear on my face as I tried to peer through the surface of the wave to identify the hazards. Thinking back, my older brother Conor and Davy Govan pioneered the peak in Bundoran when I thought they were crazy to surf somewhere so dangerous. But after that first scary drop-in at Spanish Point I was now ready for anything the wild Atlantic was going to throw at me.'

That concluded the historic European Surfing Championships of 1972, but the International Surfari to Rossnowlagh was yet to come. As said, this was run by Sam McCrum, who lamented there were only a few people on the trip. One of them was Barry Britton, who again had something to report:

'I travelled up the coast from Lahinch with another north coast local, Brian Farthing, in his soon-to-be classic Ford

Anglia – "classic", or in other words, ancient! We were hell bent on making it to Rossnowlagh for the Intercounty Surfing Championships at the end of the week – not an easy task with all the distractions and diversions to be investigated along the way.'

'Brian seemed always to be behind the wheel of our intriguing surf vehicle. One of them was a little red Fiat Bambino with the removable vinyl panel in the roof (the precursor to the sunroof!). Brian is about six feet six inches tall, and it was a tight squeeze for him to fit into the wee car. So, with his knees banging off the dashboard, he'd drive around in a World War Two Biggles outfit of flying jacket, goggles and scarf, with head and shoulders sticking out through the roof! On the way, north from Clare in the Anglia, which had a top speed of 30 m.p.h., my job was to sit in the passenger seat and make sandwiches so we wouldn't need to stop. Every hour or so we drove past all the other, more modern vehicles because they were stopped at a watering hole or refuelling – only to be passed out again by them as they zoomed on to the next pub.'

Many Brave Characters

Brian Clark was a local Bray boy who came with Ann and me on many trips. Brian became part of the furniture, and then bought a board from C&S. Sadly he was later killed in a traffic accident. Then there was Mike Kovacevich from Bakersfield, California. His Dad was Hungarian and owned a vineyard, while Mike was a teacher in a school at Lucan, Co. Dublin. During one of Mike's trips, he bought a VW van and imported it to Ireland. He realised that there were loads of surfing opportunities in Ireland, and a van was now a necessity. He brought with him a Californian-style surfer roof rack that was padded, and could divide to carry four ten-foot boards and also a pair of lace-up tan boots – lumberjack style. I gladly forked out for these prized commodities from afar. The boots helped the illusion that I was tough to deal with, and so they became my best surfari hackers – they gave me a sort of false authority. Pity I could not have worn them at work!

It is also important to record that In April 1973, three surfers from the north-west made maritime history by displaying their presence of mind in a terrifying situation. Our well-known friends, Roci Allan, David Pierce and Grant Robinson were surfing at Easkey. They noticed that the sea was getting larger by the moment and great waves were beginning to break out beyond them. As a result, they paddled out, much like Dave Kenny and I had done in Strandhill – to get beyond the break. However, these lads had to go out so far that they were swept out into Donegal Bay. The most important part of the story is that they tied themselves together with their leashes and drifted as a much more identifiable mass. The rescue helicopter caught sight of them just before dark and they were winched to safety. Their boards had to be abandoned, but the following day a local fisherman told them where the boards would be washed ashore and as luck once again had it, they found the boards – quite damaged but intact.

These episodes silently the Golden Era and first ten years of surfing in Ireland to an end. What was to follow, was just as exciting, but more professional, in every sense of the word. It would be an era of improved surfing technology and freer thinking. This departure of many to greener pastures overseas, was for a time a very sad Aloha – or was it just another bubble bursting in a health chain of events? Do read on.

Sayonara

By now our hotel had gone into receivership because of the rather radical decline in U.K and Northern Ireland tourist, these were the mainstay of our business. Also in 1965, my Father had undertaken an enormous building programme that added forty bedroom with bathrooms, a new kitchen and dining room and on top of it all, a rooftop restaurant come function room. To service all this luxury a new elevator was added and a bold neon sign on the tower announce in Las Vegas style writing, 'The Royal Starlight Hotel'. Mr Franklin of AIB South Richmond street called us to a meeting.

We felt like children under his steely leer, as he pointed out that we were about to be taken over by their accountants. By the spring of 1974, I was still with the hotel, having opted to work along with the receivers. Ann and I and family, intended immigrating to Canada and had already applied for a visa. My brother was also making his alternative plans at the time he would stay in Ireland and as the years rolled by eventually both he, and his wife Geraldine, achieved having a family of six.

It appeared that fate had stepped in to forbid my further participation with surfing. Another hex affected the sport in general as it had achieved its goals and now needed new direction. However, this would have to wait for a photo kinesis in the flower of young lives before fresh progress could be made. So many of us had folded our tents and faded into oblivion, what else was to be expected? Brian had completed his accountancy studies and secured a job in Zambia and therefore would be away for a few years to come. Roger had already departed for Kuala Lumpur. Harry Evans retired from surfing because of his workload, and thus the Surf Club of Ireland ceased to exist. Jurek was making plans to move to Geneva where he would work with IATA. Mike Murphy told us in a bulletin that the West Coast Surf Club had folded, that their club had gone into meltdown as the band of western brothers rose to new responsibilities and commitments. They had burned the candle at both ends and wanted to live to cherish the memories. These guys and girls had been the epitome of an Irish solution to a Californian problem and had cruised through it with style. These cavalier days could never be repeated because of the nature of the new world evolving around them, but they should never be forgotten. This was the end of the Golden era of Irish Surfing but hold your breath, there is more to come!

Bo Vance had the same story about the North Shore Club. He had once hoped his club would host a European event, but before that could happen it also dissolved, leaving Bo looking at a new world of surfing evolving around him:

'It saddens me a bit to see kids whose parents have bought them a few lessons in a surf school (often without a wave in sight), nice boards (maybe too small) and coloured wetsuits in the belief that this will make them into surfers.'

The only good thing intact and functioning was the Irish Surfing Association and this would be the cornerstone for a rebirth. Yet there was more to come – there were more wild geese, and I was about to meet one very soon. As we were leaving for Canada, at Dublin Airport's departure area, we met Susan Fawcett, who had manned the first club Boat Show stand with such diligence. Susan was immigrating to San Francisco, and this would do her no harm because her mother was American and she would have support from relatives over there. All this was the nature of Ireland at its worst, this was the side that we surfers never wanted to acknowledge, and perhaps the hours spent in the ocean anaesthetised us from the harsh realities now being faced by some. Ireland was like a living being, a bird in the nest shedding its young so as others could stay. Would these phenomena ever cease to happen on this lonely isle? The answer is clearly, No, it will never cease; and is likely to continue regardless of time and prosperity.

It was during all this that my brother Colm announced that he would be getting married – miracles will never cease. The cycle continues. I had got rid of all my surf gear when going to Canada, on the belief that, with California lying just south of Vancouver, its influence would be in the air. Alas, that was not the case and surfing in Canada was many years behind Ireland and in summer, the guys still wore Speedos! I got to surf Vancouver Island, probably one of the earliest, or maybe the first person, I don't know! However, it was stunning to ride the waves of Pacific Rim beaches, while looking at whales passing on the horizon. The northern Pacific midsummer waves were about four feet and quite chilly. It was strange to see that the trees that fringed the bays were pines and not palms, but this added to the unique experience. At the Tofino end of the bay he saw the Wickishine Inn hotel closed and falling into the sea, what a shame! In later years this was refurbished and became a mecca for surfers. At the Uculet end we stayed in a slam motel surrounded by an indigenous Indian population. Then we drove back through the lumber town of Port Alberni and prepared to move from Vancouver to Alberta with the compliments of the Four Seasons Hotel where I was now employed. It was there between skiing trips that our second child, Paul William, was born and altogether we were there six years. As assistant hotel manager, I was charged to look after Princes Charles and Andrew during their visit for the famous Calgary Stampede. They were both very nice to us and were prepared to engage in light conversation but also took time to meet quite a few of the associates before leaving. Despite their rather tight schedule they took one evening to stay at home. We therefore, lit a log fire in the suite and served a simple evening meal, and left them to enjoy.

It was during the following summer that I noticed people were sailing on the lakes using large surfboards with sails. The words of Sean O'Connell in Cork came to back to haunt me: 'Why don't you guys put a sail on your boards?' To which poor Sean had got a sharp reply!

I learned that in 1979, while we were away, there was an anti-Smirnoff vodka surfing contest protest. Some people climbed the castle at Easkey and displayed a huge – No Contest Here – sign. I was glad not to be around. At the time, we were skiing all over the Rockies and both my children, Carolyn and Paul, were growing proficient at the sport. In June 1980, we managed a trip to the Islands and blissfully got to surf Waikiki once again but also Lahaina in Maui. In 1981, we returned to Ireland with enough cash to buy a house and a very small car. I then commenced studying physics and philosophy in a quest to find the grand unified theory of everything. This effort eventually culminated in a book – The Republic of Paradise, which is on the web with www.trafford.com. On the surf scene, here were good things happening at last, as Eamon Matthews remembers:

'In 1978 Brian Britton returned from overseas and immediately teamed up with Roci Allan to re build Ireland on the world surfing map again. This time around it was done in a highly professional manner. These guys were serious about what they were doing. They began by going to all the overseas contests, ensuring Irish entries, and working on the ISA and European Surfing Federation bodies. Around that time some names came to the forefront of the sport: Grant Robinson from Enniskillen, who later became National Champion four times and European Masters Champion in 1987, Dave Pierce, Stan Burns, Tom Hickey, the Byrne brothers and Henry Moore from Tramore all became household surfing names. Henry rode Sunset Beach Oahu at eighteen feet and Jardim do Mar, Madeira, at fifteen, as its tubes peeled off around a steep cliff face. Youngsters such as Brian Cromie, Wesley and Ashley Moore and Graham Stinson became the second generation of North Shore surfers. Ray McDaid, Kevin McClosky, Dara Daly and the McGuinness brothers took up the challenge. Then Brian Britton subsequently invigorated the ISA in the early Eighties, and with that brought a new intensity to competition, with a place on the Irish team for international contests as an objective. I have happy memories of travelling with Brian to compete in two European contests and a World contest in France around this time. The ultimate contest experience for me had to be the World Championships on the Gold Coast of Australia in 1982. One of the great things about sport, and surfing is no different, is the long-term friendships generated between competitors. Regardless of the passage of time we still meet and after comparing our most recent scars we exchange stories, details of 'secret spots' and equipment, etc. Surf locations in any part of the world require one to be there when wind and swell coincide. The waves of Australia, California and Mexico have all been exciting and many times challenging, but the reefs of Counties Sligo and Donegal would be home to my favourite surfing breaks.'

The result of all this is that many new clubs emerged in all parts of the country and that included the re-establishment of the Lahinch

Surf Club, brought about by the Breslan family. Furthermore, all clubs from then onwards had to ensure their members with third-party liability. This was put in place by the ISA and exists to this day.

In 1982 Gerard and Declan Byrne, Lynda and Cristina, their girlfriends, and I formed the East Coast Surf Club. This was done with the assistance of Brian Britton and Zoe Lally, who came and gave the launching an air of professionalism. Gerry Collins provided a room in the Great Outdoors sports shop in Chatham Street, Dublin, for the event. It was a minor success but only lasted a year because once again there was disruption, and we all went our separate ways. After five years, working in Shannon I managed to get back to Dublin full time. There were three happy events. Firstly, we were blessed with a baby girl who we named Georgina Maria. Secondly, I ran my second marathon and lastly, a new East Coast Surf Club was formed. It happened as a result of an accidental meeting of the third kind. Our alien encounter was at a Texaco filling station on the Bray Road. It was Ann who spied him and shouted out, 'Sammy McCrum!'

Without further ado, Sam and I, now both old grey-haired ginks, reformed a new East Coast Surf Club because we were now living permanently in the area and because Surfing fever was now gripping Dublin. Gerry Collins from the Great Outdoors once again gave us the use of a room for the club launch. Johnny Lee also joined, even though by now he was not only a surfer but an ardent windsurfer and snowboarder. Sam contributed to the organising of meetings but had not surfed for quite some time. This was borne out when we finally persuaded him to try it. Not only was Sam shy about the prospect of cold waves, but to the enjoyment of all, he put on his wetsuit back to front.

By now, Gerard Byrne and Lynda had moved to live in Aughris, but the success of the new club was also partially due to the Byrnes announcing that they had remaining funds from the first club, which they passed to Zoe Lally, who presented the money to our new treasurer. This honourable act was much appreciated, and should not be forgotten. The new club is still in existence and contributes much to the surfing community and the ISA and annually helps with Surf to Heal in Tramore where Autistic children are given a days surfing.

However, this takes us to a sad turn of events that tarnished the image of our mystical island internationally. In 2001, it was announced that the World event would come to Bundoran. This announcement was premature, and therefore caused lots of local surfer to become stressed and possessive of their beaches – they did not want intruders. The ISA was faced with a dilemma, and eventually, after a failed national plebiscite of all registered members, it had to resort to a phone poll of club committees. As it turned out, the East Coast Surf Club was almost the only club that voted in favour of the event. Maybe we would not have had to shoulder the responsibility or feel the heat, but we believed the youth in the area would have benefitted, not to mention the whole community. However, as a result, France took the contest instead of Ireland. The house of cards had came tumbling down once again!

Meanwhile, in Tramore the new T Bay Surf Club was now alive and well. They in their wisdom had commissioned a state-of-the-art clubhouse, and Dave Smith, who was also a surfer, was the architect. That is why Tramore can boast of having the best surf club pavilion in Ireland, or even further afield. Some years after that I retired at sixty-five – not permitted to stay working at the Beaumont Hospital beyond that age. I met John McCarthy from Lahinch at the National Championships in Portrush who said, 'Hey, Kev! Why don't you become a Surf Instructor?'

As I had already done the ISA instructor's course administered by Tom Hickey, I was halfway there, but I still had to do the beach lifeguard course. I eventually did that in the Ennis swimming pool and White Strand and then did voluntary work with Lahinch Surf School for three summers. Afterwards, John kindly wrote:

'Thanks for your big part in bringing surfing in Ireland to where it is today. It was a complete privilege to have you hanging out in Lahinch and teaching in Lahinch Surf School during those crazy years when the surf school was getting going! I'm excited to see the shape surfing in Ireland will take on in the future. We've got the big-wave riders, we've got the surf schools stacked with groms, kids and teens and we've got lots of big people excited about the sport. It doesn't really get better than that. Hopefully we can all keep sharing the stoke and always make way for someone else on our waves. If we can do that there's great hope that Ireland will remain famous for being a friendly place to share a wave.'

CHAPTER 15

Silver Surfari at Lahinch

In 2005, Mike Moran became Men's Irish surfing champion, and in 2006 Fergal Smith took the title. In the Women's Nationals Easkey Britton was once again the winner. In that same year 2006, another event of note was to take place. This was one that needed to be recorded for posterity and another milestone in the history of the sport in Ireland. It was called the Silver Surfari and Patrons tour – a celebration and reunion of the early surfers of Ireland. It took place in October 2006 as we celebrated forty years of the sport in this island. The spadework for this event was done by Brian and Roci, with help from Ian Hill, Stan Burns, Hugh O'Brien Moran, Sam McCrum and a tad of help from me. The event was spread over two weekends and began on Friday 7th of October when the first contingent gathered in Kenny's Bar, Lahinch. Among the long-distance guests were Alan and Evelyn Rich, now living in Australia, Roger Steadman back from Kenya with his wife Halima. Also, John Boomer, Albert Harris from Wales, also attended travelling there with Dave Friar and Mike Cunningham and Steve Daniel. Locally, there was Martin Lloyd, Sam McCrum, Hugh Milne, Derek and Damian Musgrave, Wally Fogarty and Grant Robinson. Unfortunately, neither Ian Hill nor his son Andy were able to attend. Andy now carries on his father's name with pride, because not only is he a renowned surfer in his own right, but also owns a well-known sport shop in Portstewart called Trog's Surf and Fashion Store.

The Irish Times covered the event with a fine article in the sports section under the heading, 'The Boys of Summer', showing Brian and me surfing in Strandhill but also interviewing Roger Steadman and Kevin Naughton who said that when he eventually got to Ireland to surf in the mid Seventies, he found that people had copped on and the surf scene was developing. Nevertheless, he surfed all around the island and not only that, but he made surf movies of his travels abroad. As it turned out, Kevin did not know that a few years later an Irish film-maker called Joelle Conroy would make an epic Hollywood movie about the Irish–Hawaiian connection and that Kevin Naughton would be one of the main actors. It is called simply Wave Riders and proved to be a blockbuster.

When the dancing started Sam McCrum was first on the floor while Wally Fogarty sat there quite happy because he was afraid someone would shout 'Seaweed!' just for the craic. Then Tom O'Brien from Cork popped up and with so many 'non-words', demonstrated how his life had turned into a state of magnificence. Tom had a beautiful wife called Emily, who shared his disability. Yet with smiles and notebooks they chatted and then introduced their daughter Avril who winked and said in a melodious voice,

'Nice meeting you, Kevin, my parents told me about you and the other surfers.'

What a moment!

While still in Kenny's a tall lean guy in a Hawaiian shirt and an Indiana Jones hat watched the goings on from the shadows. Then at an appropriate time he introduced himself and his wife and removed his hat to display a firm face and a greying crewcut.

'Why, it's Pat Kinsella!'

Pat reminded me about some forgotten aspects of the first surfari and confirmed that he did in fact return to Cornwall, where he shaped boards. Later he became economics correspondent for RTÉ and eventually head of the Communications department in DCU. Pat was now a golfer but he enjoyed the memories of the early days.

On the following morning, Saturday, despite the celebration we were up bright and early. There was some surfing to be done and then a log surfari to Rossnowlagh and no one knows what might delay us on the way! Alan Rich arrived and prepared to surf but had to borrow a wetsuit and boots, but there was none to be had. So, with freezing twinkle toes he soldiered on. Alan later recalled his return to the chilly waters of Ireland:

'The 2006 Patrons' Pilgrimage kicked off in earnest the following morning at Lahinch. I last stood here squinting in the sun at the curiously empty lefts breaking off the southern bluffs in 1970 when these waves were virgins, but we were to change all that. There is a sense of surrealism, déjà vu, as I again scan the line-up in 2006. Today, just on the far side of a series of left reefs sits Moy Bay. It is the chosen spot to officially christen our 2006 pilgrimage as Cregg. As a sheltered cove, it is well suited to my advancing years. While the older guys size up the beach, I have my eye set on a nifty pitching right in the corner. After some protracted negotiations with my rubber armament, I optimistically borrow one of 71-year-old Johnny Lee's newer boards and paddle out. It's a mere fourteen years old, the ex-jet pilot reckons.' Alan continues,

'The tides in Lahinch are big, ranging through 4.3 metres this weekend, which means my good right, a surf spot fifteen minutes ago, is now almost gone. My sights shift to the next break down, one of those lefts from yesteryear, which seems to grow larger with each set. The difference in swell size just a hundred metres away is dramatic. It's like Bartra Point on the earlier tide this morning – sizeable, clean, and unwinding. Kevin Cavey and I paddle into the line-up from the back door. I've waited thirty-six years for this. Almost immediately a wave too good to miss appears with my name on it, and I'm paddling from the pole position without thinking. As the peak jacks overhead, Johnny's old board slides in and I accelerate into a drawn-out backside wall. It's then, spying the boils ahead that I finally wake up to myself. I've just broken the surf traveller's basic rule: check it out first. I've never even seen a wave break here, and I don't know where I'm going. Plus, I'm on a borrowed board. So what do you do? You just keep going, as far as I could, and hope for the luck of the Irish. And so, I'm thinkin', this is shaping up to be a fine week, to be sure.'

It was time for the surfari wagons to roll. Roger and his wife Halima led the way, followed by Alan and his wife Evelyn then there was Hugh and Niall O'Brien Moran and me. Alan is a on the Ballina New South Wales Council and as it turned out, he and Evelyn were invited for lunch in Ballina (Ireland) as guests of the Mayo County Council. After the lunch, Evelyn told us with a chuckle,

'When Alan was asked to explain the Irish connection with Ballina, NSW, he blundered, "Sorry, but it's not, it's an Aborigine name!"'

Alan had no need to be embarrassed as surfers would never worry about faux pas, but we enjoyed the yarn.

Barry Britton, one of the pilgrims, tells his story of the week:

'The Silver Surfari of 2006 was a commemorative journey up the coast from Lahinch to Rossnowlagh (in commemoration of the first 1966 surfari to Sligo and Donegal) for old salty dogs like us. All this was in keeping with the early days because, if my memory serves me well, I seem to recall that the Limerick Leader Surf Competition would be held at Lahinch towards the end of season and the Intercounties would be on the following weekend, thus allowing for an annual week-long surfari. For this Silver Surfari, I set out in reverse going from Rossnowlagh with the best intentions to hit Lahinch before the weekend – I just thought I'd go around and check Easkey on the way. Well, it turned out the waves were very nice and there weren't too many interlopers about.

It has always been my number one rule – never drive away from good surf! So, I was to be found still there towards the end of the following week. It was then that the whole Silver Surfari crew breezed through and joined in the fun. Aye, old habits die hard!'

Silver Surfari at Rossnowlagh

With surfing finished at Creg the surfari headed to Rossnowlagh via Balina, Easkey and Lisadell and eventually arrived at the Sandhouse Hotel, many for the first time in forty years. It was still Saturday, 14th October 2006 but unfortunately some people could not make both weekends and some could not make it at all. Jurek, though alive and well, was one who could not make the event. He is living with wife and family in Leitrim following many years in Switzerland. Colm was also not available as he was away at the time.

Once checked into the Hotel we linked up with those who missed the beginning of the trip at Lahinch. Among the older group was Tom Flynn, who had been the backbone of the Fastnet SC and 1972 Europeans in Lahinch. Tom and his wife returned from England for the reunion. The well-known Kevin Naughton was also there, and as usual he had been out cutting up the waves from Easkey to Lisadell as he journeyed north. Other old timers were, Rodney Sumpter who was by now the author of several well-known surfing books, Mike Cunningham, Dave Friar and Craig Petersen from the UK, but also Dave, Niall and Greg Kenny had also arrived in a traditional camper with boards strapped on top. The event was also supported by members of the more recent East Coast Surf Club.

Brian Britton

Brian Britton, during the Silver Surfari at Rossnowlagh in 2006

Also, there was the renowned lady Carmel Evans, with daughter Vivienne, who had returned from Miami where she now lives. Carmel said, in a shaken voice, she fondly remembered the days when they as a family stayed in Mrs Barrett's B&B in Lahinch. Here they had the best of both worlds, sand for the kids and surf for the older ones. Harry (who had now passed away) used to take the family to all parts of Ireland in search of a wave. One day he surprised the family by selling his family car for a two-seat sports model instead. This meant that the young ones just had to take the train. Carmel now looked like she had visited the past as she sat in Mary Britton's hotel lounge, quite dazzled and emotional at the sight of the old faces tumbling in the door, but of course her hero, Harry, could not be there! However, Harry was being honoured in spirit that weekend as one of three deceased Patrons. The other two were Dr O'Brien-Moran and Vinnie Britton.

That evening there was a memorial dinner in the Sandhouse where Brian was delighted to announce that their hotel had received the AA double rosettes 2006 good food award. There was applause and agreement all around the room. Then he said, with a glint in his eye, how the idea first came to him. He said it was around two or three in the morning, and he was having a pint of Guinness with Roci – a few pints actually. He paused, grinning at his understatement. Then he continued,

'And I thought, why not get everybody together from the old days? Have a big reunion? Celebrate forty years of Irish surfing and honour those recently departed patrons who had supported us all. Let it be a pilgrimage for the patrons, wouldn't that be grand? My friend Roci approved, saying sure and they won't see much o' each other these days, and if only the two o' them turn up, they'll share a couple o' pints together. Anybody after that's a bonus. What began that night between two friends and some Guinness is now at fruition.'

'The patrons were those stalwarts who lent guidance and gave support in the early days to this new fad called 'surfing' which afflicted their families and friends, if not necessarily themselves. Their kids and grandkids were now scattered at tables throughout the room. In recent years, three of these patrons had passed on and were being particularly honoured: Doc O'Brien-Moran from the Irish south coast, Dubliner Harry Evans, and Vinnie 'The Boss' Britton from Rossnowlagh in the north-west, the departed patriarch of the Britton clan.'

Following that, on behalf of the ISA, Sceach (Michael) Kelly from Tramore presented Brian with a new surfboard for his hammering together such a wonderful evening. Sceach had been and still is an invaluable element in Irish surfing, because not only was he filled with enthusiasm but he also was instrumental in the building of the new Tramore Bay Surf Club pavilion some years before. Sceach and others put their necks on the line and deserve a lot of credit for their courage.

It was a time for reflection, both on the history of surfing in Ireland and its present and future. Many of those who were there have kindly sent me their thoughts, some of which I have included here. Eamon Matthews wasn't up to the surfing itself, as he explains:

'I was sorry to have missed most of the Silver Surfari in 2006 as a result of meeting work head on, having just returned from a two-month sailing trip. I did manage to make the last weekend in Rossnowlagh, which was a blast. Walking into the foyer of the Sandhouse Hotel on that Friday evening was indeed a steep drop down memory lane! Unfortunately, two broken ribs prevented my participation in the water-based activities of the weekend.'

He went on to ponder the changes that have come over surfing through the decades:

'Surfing in Ireland has reached a popularity level which I would never have anticipated. The contributing factors are many, but gone are the days of the bemused looks from passers-by when pointing at the 'looneys' stripping off their clothes on a wet and windy winter afternoon. This development of interest in surfing has brought so many new and talented participants to the sport and to a whole new level of performance on the waves. The exploitation of the hairier big waves offshore will be a story in itself and must now be the main ambition of the most capable of the current crew.

'From a personal point of view, I have come to realise how privileged I am to have been able to surf those beaches and reefs over the years alone or with a couple of friends. Those days are gone, it's a different experience now – lots of fun but not so much soul. That sense of intimacy between man and natural force is at least diluted.'

Linda and Ger Byrne were among the pilgrims at Rossnowlagh. For them, the family surfing tradition is maintained by their daughter, Ione Byrne. She sent me this reflection on the family's surfing life:

'Living with a surfing family is cool. I guess people think it might be difficult or unusual but when you grow up experiencing and surfing all your life, it just seems normal. Everything has always been built around the sport – where we go on holidays, work, college, everything. My Dad has been a builder of boards since the late Sixties but also, would you believe, he builds our campers so that we regularly go at Christmas to Spain, Portugal, France, Morocco and even California. The highlight of it all was when I was ten we stayed six months in Portugal, close to a beach, and I went to the local school.

'It all started when I was four and had my first bodyboard in Enniscrone. Soon after that I found a big piece of polystyrene in Easkey, and made my Dad shape it into a surfboard that I could stand on. While still only five or six I became tired of being pounded in the shorebreak at Dunmoran, so I just paddled outside where it was calmer. Needless to say, from then on, I began to catch green walls and my surfing began to happen. When the surf is pumping we usually scramble to get all our gear in the van and it is only when the three of us hit the water that tension eases, and for the rest of the day everyone is mellow and in a happy disposition. Eventually by twelve years of age I went on to compete in the European Surfing Championships and though I am twenty-one now I still surf, and always will. Surfing is a lifestyle – even my dog surfs – and therefore a job in a city working nine to five will just never appeal.'

Zoe Lally commented,

'The 2006 Silver Surfari was inspirational, I got some great photos. It was lovely watching Gwyn Haslock surfing, I had met her many years before in Cornwall. I also got a great wipe-out photo of Linda Byrne that I have been using to blackmail her with ever since.'

Roci Allan, who had done so much to make the Silver Surfari happen, told me about the friendships that the sport has brought him:

'Thirty-five years of surfing has given me many good friends around the world, from Owen Hooper in Australia to Francis Distinguin in France, to Robin de Koch in South Africa, to Lily Pires in Brazil, and so on ad infinitum. My closest friends in surfing, however, that still remain great friends today, were made in that first year of surfing in 1971: Dave and Olly Pierce, and Hugh and Margaret O'Brien-Moran.'

Next day, Sunday 15th, Brian's daughter Naomi, who was now in the media business, was making a documentary for RTÉ called the Silver Surfari. This was made into a DVD and can be bought in most surf shops today. Naomi is also a surfer, displaying all the trimmings of one reared in the Britton surfing ethos. She is tall, elegant and a great ambassador of the sport. Around the same time as this Ken O'Sullivan in Lahinch made a similar movie that showed Easkey Britton tow-in surfing at Aileens. It is called Sea Fever.

Then fully decked in wetsuits and carrying their oldest boards, the band of twenty-five surfing brothers lined up for a photograph before entering the sea.

They were left to right; Linda Byrne, Gwyn Haslock, Dave Moynihan, Gerard Byrne, Martin Lloyd, Terry Mc Laughlen, Dorian Mc Laughlin, Bob Haslock, Alan Rich, Roger Steadman, Kevin Cavey, Kevin Naughton, Stan Burns, Greg Kenny, Dave Kenny, Derek Musgrave, Damian Musgrave, Tom O'Brien, David Nagle, William Britton, Brian Britton, Roci Alan, Hugh O'Brian Moran, Steve Daniel, and Ted Alexander.

At the word from Sceach they all entered the sea and began to paddle out into waves of about four feet to perform for the public. However, there was more to it because these guys and girls were doing what they do best and were proud to be in each other's company. Sceach gave a rousing commentary and the rides were spectacular, large carving turns, nose rides accompanied by whoops and hollers. Then two ancient mariners shared a wave and without complaining both Kevin Naughton and Steve Daniel rode skilfully to shore. I shared a wave with Brian Britton and we rode to shore singing in pure delight. We sang different songs but it did not matter. I was singing Aloha 'Oe (Queen Lili 'uokalani) but Brain was somewhere in the middle of Guns and Roses. Then I paddled out once again and stopped to listen to the banter. Sure enough, there they were, all the old names once again.

'Hey, Roger, here comes a good one – outside – regarde la!'

'Hey, Dave, Johnny, nice wave. Hughie, Grant, where you bin? Barry, you have this place wired. Hi Gwyn your wave. Hey Ted, Niall, Bo, common we'll all grab the next one – a party wave, why not!'

Sunset on a great day. Rossnowlagh 2006

CHAPTER 16

Tow-ins

John Mc Carthy, at this stage had become a tow-in surfer because he was awestruck by the concept of someone being pulled onto a wave already standing without having to paddle. He teamed up with a fellow Tramore surfer called Dave Blount and between them bought a jet ski and proper tow-in boards. They began their quest by riding a wave call *"Aill Na Searrach"* or *"Aillens" for short* at the cliffs of moher. Richard Fitzgerald from Bundoran is also a tow-in surfer from the very start, and his pet wave was a gigantic winter monster off the headland of Mullaghmore – he too was a man literally in motion. Other icons of the new tow-in era to only name two, is Fergal Smith and Al Meenie both who get regularly written in magazines for they are also a new breed of fearless beings. It was all started by the famous American, Laird Hamilton in Kauai, at a place called Jaws. Now countless people are making the investment, and doing the same thing around the country as they access reefs that were unknown before. Some of these people include Peter Conroy, Glyn Ovens, Alastair Mennie, Andrew Cotton, Gabe Davies, Mikee Hamilton and Dave Lavelle. Yet, to most people's disbelief, there is a young woman who is also a tow-in surfer. She is Barry Britton's daughter, Easkey Britton. Not only does she get towed onto waves of over thirty feet, but she is a surfboard rider of great ability. Easkey has maintained a balanced life by achieving academic qualification at Coleraine University, but also managed to win the Nationals from 2005 to 2008.

Now, bearing all this excitement in mind in mind, I also had an ambition to be towed onto a wave. For me it would have to be small, say about fifteen feet, but I have a lazy streak and being towed in has appeal. By the grace of King Neptune and the Good Lord himself, in January 2007 I got another surprise. While at work in the Shelbourne Hotel, Dublin, I got a call from a girl called Nieve of Liberty Films in Dublin. She established who I was and then said,

'If you went to Australia what would be your wish?'

'Why, Nieve, I would like to be towed onto large wave by jet-ski. Gulp!'

She said they were making a six-part series called 'Your wish before you die.' Their originally selected person for a shark cage dive in Australia had fallen ill. They need a replacement.

Then Nieve asked, 'What is a Tow-in work?'

So I explained and Nieve said, 'Wow, that sounds exciting but we will have to check with the insurance company as this is quite different, but can you be ready to fly to Brisbane in a five days' time?' As is turned out, the insurance company dictated that the waves could not be over ten feet and we asked could we please do it at eighteen, and they settled for fifteen – what a laugh.

I finally got a Tow–in at Currumbin Alley in Queensland in about eight-foot waves, just a shadow of the real thing, but it was still a great experience. Later there was a surprise dinner scheduled with Alan Rich and his wife Evelyn. All this got on film and was shown on RTE in the following summer.

ISA Today

The Irish Surfing Association remains the voice of surfing in Ireland, but is also answerable to the clubs around the country. Much of its success is due to the dedicated efforts of its development officer, Zoe Lally women's Irish surfing champion on thirteen occasions. Over the years Zoe has single handedly managed the many complex issues and administered over surfing's many events. Besides that she remains to this day as one of Ireland's best female surfers. Today, there are approximately 50,000 surfers in Ireland and the ISA comprises 2,500 members and twenty surf clubs, each representing a different geographic location or surfing ethos. With more surfers in Ireland than ever before, the surf industry is booming. There are approximately forty surf schools and a similar number of surf shops. The ISA is still faced with the challenge of balancing the views of Irish surfers on issues such as competition, commercialisation and publicity, along with contemporary issues such as environment, overcrowding and increased safety concerns.

To achieve all this the ISA must provide third-party insurance for their clubs and members, monitor beach access, intervene in support of planning objections to harbour enlargements, be representative on sports councils and above all be in close contact with the Irish Water Safety Association and all maritime county councils. They assemble the annual calendar of events, and ensure that they are carried out in a properly organised way, and in accordance with the judging rules of the association.

There would also be negotiations about a new body called the Irish Tow and Surf Rescue Club, which has been set up on a voluntary basis to improve safety within our sport, but we are also keen to formalise procedures. Then they must accommodate the new stand-up paddleboarders, as they also have competitions. Then there is the assembly of the Irish squads competing overseas; here again there is another responsibility that remains till the teams return safely home. By 2020 they will return home from far strung places. For now we are faced with the likelihood of surfing becoming an Olympic sport! The ramifications of this leap are enormous as the sort should from then onwards be looked on as something for young people to strive for. Surfing will then take its place a power to be reckoned with – a true sport of Kings.

Last, but not least, they observe the many charitable undertakings that surfing is now involved in. The ISA publicises events on its web site such as the Tramore Legends annual presentation for old timers, also the Cork-based Surf2Heal, for autistic children which is run in several places around Ireland. Clubs such as the East Coast Surf Club rally up to fifty volunteers annually for four days to chaperone and introduce these children to surfing. The event is usually centred at Billy Butler's Freedom Surf School. The ISA also gives publicity to clubs who raise money for cystic fibrosis and to the newly formed Christian Surfers, who specialise in giving warm drinks to those who braved the chilly waves, keeping body and soul together – a godly act.

In Conclusion

In the introduction, we compared surfing with the forces of nature, and the result of our enslavement to kinetic energy. However, when all is said and done, many people striving for a deeper meaning will come face to face with the question 'Who created us?' Whether agnostic, Hindu or Muslim, existence is a question of mere energy for some people and God for others – acceptance or denial. Both such stances require personal courage, which leaves the undecided with a foot firmly in both camps. As Christianity has been the first and largest religion to associate itself with surfing in the west, it is felt that an acknowledgement of this support needs to be aired. Who else could explain the beauty of their message better than John McCarthy, the founder of the already mentioned, Christian Surfers Church in Lahinch:

'Mixing surfing and Christianity must seem like a strange thing! Surfing in its essence is about personal stoke, the joy of catching your perfect wave. Christianity on the other hand is about denying yourself and laying down your life for the greater good and of course for God. What's cool is when a surfer's heart gets transformed by God and by the realisation that the maker of the waves wants to have a close personal relationship. Jesus talked about 'knowing God' by simply trusting in the Son – like you can actually know God! Ultimately in my life that has been the greatest rush that is out there, yes even better than surfing a huge wave! As a Christian surfer, that changes everything and remarkably, the focus comes off 'self' and onto the Eternal One. Well, it's bound to be good to have a few surfers with that focus around and hopefully Christian Surfers do that.'

In September 18th, 2017, there will be a Legends reunion for the 50 years since the first Contest in 1867, let there be fun!

In 2020 there should be an Irish entry for the first ever Surfing Olympic Games, let there be success!

In September 2022, there should be a re union in Lahinch for the Europeans of 1972 however by then, it will be for a few less legends but, let there still be fun!

APPENDIX

Looking at a map of Ireland the places discussed are clockwise, as follows;

Malin Head, North coast. **Portrush,** Co Antrim on the North coast. **Magheramore** and **Brittas Bay,** Co Wicklow, just south of Dublin. **Tramore,** Co Waterford, South East coast. **Innchydoney,** West Cork, South coast. **Barley Cove,** West Cork, extreme South West coast. **Waterville,** Co Kerry, South West coast. **Lahinch,** Co Clare, West coast. **Achill Island,** West coast. **Enniscrone,** Co Mayo, also **Easkey, Aughris Quay** and **Strandhill,** are Co Sligo, on the North West coast. **Bundoran,** Co Donegal, North West coast. **Rossnowlagh,** Co Donegal, North West. **Ardara** and **Cruit Island,** Co Donegal, North West Coast. **Ballymastocker** North West coast.

Also;

ISA Irish National Surfing Champions over the years

Year	Venue	Men's Champion	Women's Champion
1967	Dublin	Kevin Cavey	
1968	Down	Ted Alexander	
1969	Waterford	Alan Duke	
1970	Antrim	Hugh O'Brien-Moran	
1971	Antrim	Derek Musgrave	

197

1972	Antrim	Alan Duke	
1973	Antrim	Derek Musgrave	
1974	Antrim	Alan Duke	
1975	Antrim	Alan Duke	
1976	Fermanagh	Grant Robinson	
1977	Waterford	William Britton	
1978	Antrim	William Britton	
1979	Derry	Grant Robinson	
1980	Antrim	William Britton	
1981	Waterford	Grant Robinson	Grace O'Sullivan
1982	Donegal	Hugh O'Brien-Moran	Margaret O'Brien
1983	Fermanagh	Hugh O'Brien-Moran	Emily Moore
1984	Waterford	Hugh O'Brien-Moran	Emily Moore
1985	Donegal	Michael Vance	Emily Moore
1986	Donegal	Kevin Tobin	Margaret O'Brien-Moran
1987	Donegal	Kevin Tobin	Margaret O'Brien-Moran
1988	Donegal	Hugh O'Brien-Moran	Zoe Lally
1989	Donegal	Andrew Hill	Zoe Lally
1990	Donegal	Andrew Hill	Zoe Lally
1991	Donegal	Andrew Hill	Jill Murphy
1992	Fermanagh	Andrew Hill	Zoe Lally
1993	Donegal	Andrew Hill	Zoe Lally
1994	Donegal	Andrew Hill	Zoe Lally
1995	Donegal	Darren Twomey	Zoe Lally
1996	Leitrim	Darren Twomey	Zoe Lally
1997	Leitrim	Joe McNulty	Zoe Lally
1998	Sligo	Colin O'Hare	Zoe Lally
1999	Waterford	Colin O'Hare	Zoe Lally
2000	Waterford	Conn McDermott	Zoe Lally
2001	Donegal	Colin O'Hare	Alexandra Monteith
2002	Waterford	Colin O'Hare	Zoe Lally
2003	Donegal	Stephen Conwell	Nicole Morgan
2004	Waterford	Cain Kilcullen	Shauna Ward

2005	Donegal	Mike Morgan	Easkey Britton
2006	Waterford	Fergal Smith	Easkey Britton
2007	Waterford	Mike Morgan	Easkey Britton
2008	Sligo	Cain Kilcullen	Easkey Britton
2009	Donegal	Fergal Smith	Nicole Morgan
2010	Sligo	Stephen Kilfeather	Nicole Morgan
2011	Sligo	Stephen Kilfeather	Easkey Britton
2012	Sligo	Ronan Oertzen	Shauna Ward
2013	Donegal	Geroid Mc Daid	Sophie Pigot
2014	Donegal	Stephen Kilfeather	Shauna Ward
2015	Tyrone	Geroid Mc Diad	Sophie Pigot
2016	Donegal	Geroid Mc Daid	Shauna Ward
2017	Laois	Gearoid Mc Daid	Una Britton
2018	Sligo	Stephen Kilfeather	Holly Widger
2019	Waterford	Rory Touhy	Una Britton
2020	In Memory of Conor Britton	No Event- Covid 19	No Event- Covid 19
2021	Waterford	No Event- Covid 19	No Event- Covid 19
2022	Sligo	Gearoid McDaid	Maia Monaghan

Printed in the United States
by Baker & Taylor Publisher Services